This Gloryland

Shelley Owen,

For warm friend friend

This Gloryland

Drew Signor

VANTAGE PRESS
New York

"Patagonia" (p. 51) and "To Be Movin' " (p. 124) have been published by Vincent Montana Jr. Music ASCAP, 1981. All rights reserved. Used with permission.

FIRST EDITION

Published by Vantage Press, Inc.
516 West 34th Street, New York, New York 10001

Manufactured in the United States of America
ISBN: 0-533-13868-X

Library of Congress Catalog Card No.: 01-126514

0 9 8 7 6 5 4 3 2 1

To my father, John J. Signor,
who was forever in love with the sound of words and
their meaning.

"This is the place our parents never warned us about. The hot ground where if you enter, you can never leave. Drew Signor shows us the way to leave the house and find our place. The heat, rock and white light that burn this place into our minds and flesh bring forth many songs. Listen up, as one lover explores the heartbreak hotel of our dreams."

—Charles Bowden

Note:
Charles Bowden is the author of *Blue Desert, Frog Mountain Blues, Mezcal, Red Line, Desierto, Blood Orchid*, and *Killing the Hidden Waters*.

Contents

This Gloryland

This Gloryland

In the shadows of the first morning's light
When the sunbeams cut the canyons
From a deep-dyed blue
Ragged mountains poke their heads
Through the porcelain clouds
And the sun's fire sparks their glow and the newborn day
Wild rivers sing their songs
And the birds they sing along in harmony
The rewards of walking this wilderness . . .
This Gloryland.

It's work but worth it as you wander this wild ground
The soothing silence stirs the soul
For the challenge of the call
Dreamscapes of color on a canvas of constant change
Timeless theatrics in this theater
That the Lord set in play
How long do mountains stand . . . how long
This beauty and the unexplained that leads me on
The rewards of walking this wilderness. . . .
This Gloryland.

I know that urban minds don't understand
Sierras packed with snow this grand
That feed these streams where lion seek their quarry
Or the starry nights that burn and blaze
Beyond this creeping city maze
That kills this Gloryland to leave us sorry
And I am the voice of one singing in this wilderness
What God has made let no man put asunder.

1

In the evenings when the gleaming sun shafts play
On the saddles and the peaks
Seared with the last dazzling beam
Retreating ranges cool their colors
In a purple parade
Clouds brightly bleeding pull the curtain
On the sun's passion play
Then constellations sing and shine
And a campfire will keep you fine until the dawn
The rewards of walking this wilderness. . . .
This Gloryland
This Gloryland.
1988

California poppies, Tollhouse Canyon, Pelloncillo Mountains.

Westward Bound

Westward bound . . . there's a peace I've found
On a road that's westward bound. . . .
On a road that's westward bound.

I've always been one to roam and wander. . . .
And I guess its always gonna be that way
Born for some rim-rock and a river with a bend
Empty deserts fenced with snowy mountain crowns.

I want a road that's westward bound. . . .
I need a prairie rolling gold or green
I need big mountains that can frame my horizons
With cutting canyons where the cataracts sound
I want a road that's westward bound.

Westward bound . . . there's a peace I've found. . . .
On a road that's westward bound
With the engine wound. . . . you'll be glory bound. . . .
On any road just west of town
On a road that's westward bound.

I've always been one to roam and wander. . . .
It's a call I can't describe or explain
So the spirit summons and this gypsy can't remain
It's a pilgrim's ceaseless search for Holy ground.

I want a road that's westward bound. . . .
I need a prairie rolling gold or green
I need big mountains that can frame my horizons
With quiet canyons graced with cottonwood down
I want a road that's westward bound.

Westward bound . . . there's a peace I've found. . . .
On a road that's westward bound
So if I'm not around. . . . I'm sure to wander. . . .
I'm bound
For any road just west of town.

Westward bound . . . there's a peace I've found. . . .
On a road that's westward bound
On a road that's westward bound. . . .
On a road that's westward bound.
1997

San Rafael Grasslands, east of Patagonia.

Summer Rain

In the evenings after dinner as the day draws to a close, I step out my door, cross Sonoita Creek, and climb a small hill, to watch the setting sun. From this vantage point, I can look out across our peaceful pastoral valley and the town of Patagonia. Blue mountains fence the horizon. The rippling roll of grassy hills determines the creek's cottonwooded course through a perfect hollow.

That vault of blue sky and its cloud-colored splendor, with the last pure rays of sunlight, paint a mixture of pigment across the firmament of such transcendent glory that only seeing would be believing. Each evening I see, and yet cannot believe, that such a landscape of poetry, such radiant light, exists outside heaven itself.

No clever manipulation of vocabulary, no manner of linguistic craftiness, could begin to define the keen colors that hang each evening in the clean atmosphere or describe what this beauty does to my spirit. To put it simply, rather than struggle for words I cannot find, it makes me want to go walking, to walk endlessly onward.

For most of the year, this pastoral landscape is painted in golden hues, but with the coming of summer rains, grass carpets are transformed from a thing already handsome, into succulent neon green pastures filled with flowers and steeped in the fragrances of summer.

I guess one is always surprised with the change of seasons. Not that they will change, but that they are always more lovely than we remember them. But the emerald prairie grasses that stretch out before me, that roll like a Kansas sea of wheat, rank and dark, falls on the retina with a genuine surprise. I stare at this landscape and the canopy of colored clouds strewn across the heavens, believing that such light and color cannot exist outside some drug-induced state. The truth is stranger than fiction.

It is nothing more than summer. Though more beautiful than summers past, it is nothing more than summer, beautiful summer.

A Heart in Two Places

It's been so long I don't recall
Just when I felt the road first called my name
But there's just somethin' in this restless soul
And those I love no doubt complain
But I feel the need to be a wanderin' somewhere
So I hope this song explains
Cause I've got a heart. . . .
I've got a heart in two places.

Sometimes I wonder how it came to be
Me lovin' trains . . . the road . . . and topography
This endless yearnin' in my heart to free
These songs that flow from deep inside of me
Still every callin' has its heartache
Every wanderer is lonesome. . . .
Every cowboy's missin' home
And I've got a heart. . . .
I've got a heart in two places.

I guess you let a restless heart roam a while
The open road a sojourner's domicile. . . .
No way to reconcile
The folks you love and the dreams that call
And I've got a heart . . . I got a heart in two places
Broken in two places.

Its been so long I don't recall
Just when I felt the road first called my name
But there's just somethin' in this restless soul
And those I love no doubt complain
But I feel the need to be a wanderin' somewhere
So I hope this song explains
'Cause I've got a heart. . . .
I've got a heart in two places
Broken in two places . . . in two places.
1984

Buehman Creek, Santa Catalina Mountains.

Beautiful Things

Arizona is at least as much a place in my head, as it is a place in reality. But the reality is so rewarding, and it is the foundation on which I have set a large portion of my life.

All I ever wanted to do was to write songs and take a walk somewhere. The world is not interested in such craziness. Walking Arizona has provided me an unending adventure and a wellspring of song-writing inspiration. It is a place steeped in an eternal beauty, an undying mystery. It is a theater for the imagination. I have let my feet and my mind wander.

I am the least practical person I ever met, as evidenced from the fact that I am on my fourth decade of writing songs, with the full knowledge that no amount of talent, determination, or dogged pursuit of my goal can bring this dream to fruition as a working reality. I remain undaunted for one reason only. It is a natural calling; I wouldn't know who I was if I couldn't pick up a guitar. I have pursued my craft with an honest and pure heart, for the sheer love and joy of doing it.

I have pursued walking with the same enthusiasm, for the same reasons. It is a natural calling; I wouldn't know who I was, if I couldn't take a walk. For me there has always been an inherent emotional and spiritual response to landscape, which pulls me into it like gravity. Any interesting landscape would do. Preferably a Western landscape, but if I lived in Scotland or Spain in Appalachia or Argentina, or name the place, my life would be the same. I would be walking and fashioning songs. The walking and the writing go hand in hand like a marriage.

The adventure of walking lends itself to romanticism. The glory of creation lends itself to spiritual inspiration. The act of walking brings a clear mind. My natural joyous response to all this beauty is a spontaneous melody.

Fortunately, the artist has license to create out of things around

10

him, that which he will. Living in Arizona has given me a lot to work with, a large and diverse canvas from which to draw. But the wonderful world I have created in my own imagination is at least as real, as the real wonderful world, and sometimes it's quite hard for me to distinguish between the two.

Sadly, there are things I dislike about the place as well, things I wish I could change, but my impractical artistic outlook allows me to overlook the unpleasant and see only the beautiful. The futility of writing songs, now and then, comes and slaps me upside the head, and this disquieting realization proves to me how much I am living in a province of my own fabrication and how much there is I cannot reconcile.

Arizona remains an extraordinary place for an extraordinary number of reasons, and for all those reasons, I love it with my whole heart. I was born for the place. I am certain that if you took out of the equation my love for singing and writing songs, this walking, and Arizona itself, my life would cease to exist. At least as I have known it or ever wanted it to be.

This book is a collection of some of my tales, some of my lyrics, and some photographs I've taken along the way.

I boast of no talent but a great love. I am a simple man in every way and in every respect. Writing this strikes me as a bit pretentious. I must humbly consider myself a singer/songwriter, wilderness wanderer, and resident theologian. Being Swedenborgian in my outlook explains quite a bit.

I am certainly not a historian, scientist, biologist, botanist, or geologist. I have always been less concerned about the specific statistics and facts about a thing, though undeniably important, than the inherent truth and spirit of things. But all these subjects very much interest me. And as they relate to the topic at hand, I could recommend a hundred books that would be informative. I can bring nothing to the table in this regard.

This book is not about any place in particular, though every chapter is about a particular place. It is certainly not a book about maps, or what road to take, what trail to walk, what mountains to climb in. The local bookstore can provide twenty good reads in this department.

Writing provides an excuse to talk about beautiful things, the

11

art of this creation, and a passing note on the spiritual implications of landscape.

Apart from the singularly striking and uncommon components that make this a magical place, I love Arizona first and foremost, for the art of the place, the sheer aesthetics of this creation. It is the color of the air and the light in the canyons. I am less an artist, than I am one who appreciates good art and sees it in most everything. From the exultant to the mundane, everything in my eye has an aesthetic purposeful balance. And like all good art, everything is wrapped in metaphor and the more I look, the more I see.

If you want to kill a party or a friendship, you can bring up theology. Everyone is so fixed in what he or she believes and so convinced the other guy is full of it, that all you end up with is a fight. This wearies me terribly. Relax; I'm not an evangelist. I write to convince no one of anything, but to express what it is that so moves me in regards to landscape. And this passing thought that has so enhanced my appreciation of nature and has lifted my mind above the merely natural things placed before me, which in and of themselves, are marvelous and remarkable beyond words.

There is more to God than I'll ever know. In his infinite love and wisdom, his purpose is complex and manifold and yet surprisingly simple. But in regards to the art of landscape, I make this statement of which I remain quite certain: nothing works as well as creation and does not have God in it. It is the artist's job to express and to comment on this truth and the scientists to prove it. Many will laugh or scoff at my naiveté. But for those who believe, there are more than enough proofs from which to build a foundation of faith and for those who do not, all the proofs in the world are not enough.

It is no coincidence that every civilization and every religion around the world looks up at the mountain and sees its god there. I maintain, though this is by no means original thought, that it is because there is an inherent spiritual correspondence with the natural formation, which is a metaphor reflecting a deeper spiritual reality.

The stumbling block comes when you start believing that the natural object is worthy of worship, or that God actually resides there, no more than an artist who creates something beautiful, resides in the thing he has fashioned. But it is clearly reflective of every intent and purpose of its maker.

If great artists use metaphor to tell a deeper story, then surely the Greatest Artist, the source from which all things spring and in whom we live and move and have our being, has fashioned nature in such a way, apart from the obvious purposeful practicalities of creation, and if understood in its proper light, as a kind of spiritual metaphor, to reveal a higher truth. If we could lift this material veil, we would then see clearly that in every created thing, there is something reflecting our creator, his purpose, and ourselves as well. "For all nature, is a theater representative of the Lord's Kingdom."

I'm convinced as well that everyone knows this innately, without talking about it. It is and it isn't explicit. We sense it in nature, it is almost palpable, and yet it doesn't quite enter the mind. Sometimes until a statement is made on a given subject, it doesn't become a tangible idea on which the mind can rest.

Just as music is pure emotion put to melody and the emotional response to it moves us to the core of our being, and as great art lifts the spirit and the mind of man to a higher purpose, beyond himself, so the art of this masterful creation is doing the same. And this spiritual tugging at our hearts and our emotional response to beautiful things, as when we stand by a river, or walk through a forest, or look up at the mountain, is both a conscious and unconscious, reciprocal interplay between the creator and the created.

"If mountains reflect celestial love and the hills below them, the spiritual; if natural water corresponds to spiritual truth; if rocks signify faith; if animals reflect varying affections and the trees, perception and knowledge; birds, intellectual things; if gardens and groves and parks, intelligence," then landscape becomes a stage on which everything is a metaphor reflecting his purpose, like an image in a mirror, a place where natural mountains and rivers, are spirit condensed.

This grand sweep and wide array of diversified landscapes that Arizona has to offer makes this school of thought all the more dramatically pronounced and poignant.

I don't want to belabor the point. If things are beautiful just because they are beautiful, then so be it. I am so intensely and affectionately moved by this splendid artful creation and I can't help but see deeper spiritual things within, the more I gaze into this natural painting. This pleases my spirit no end and makes me think and ponder beautiful things.

Though I was born here in spirit, like everyone else, I came from another place, Pennsylvania. But I'll soon be here a quarter century, and this makes me a native. I feel I know the place well, at least the part beyond the road.

I spent most of my time residing in Tucson and San Manuel, though I spent an extraordinary year in Patagonia. I was Thoreau with a guitar. Fighting wildfires for the state, writing some wonderful songs, and walking every inch of Santa Cruz County. I have also drifted back and forth at times to the East Coast, both to earn some money and in pursuit of my mythical music career.

I walked long and hard across Arizona for ten years. Never kept a journal, because I was so intent upon writing songs and so believed, as I still do, that I could translate my love into something tangible both for myself and an audience, the grand illusion. So a lot of good walks got away without ever being recorded. After a decade I wrote a few things down just for the practice and a few of these I share with you now. The chapters were written at the time the walks were taken. It hardly matters when, because apart from where the cities are destroying it, this Gloryland remains timeless.

In reviewing these journals, I got to thinking and remembering all the places I've been and walked. It's amazing how far you can get, if you just put one foot in front of another.

In a four-month segment in 1992, I had walked and climbed in eleven different mountain ranges. Logged ninety miles traversing three different desert river systems. Nearly froze to death in the conifer forests atop the Guadalupes in west Texas and visited the Pinacate in Mexico. I have sustained this kind of pace for over twenty years. It has not seemed at all like a marathon, but a steady plodding along for the sheer wonder and joy of it.

The bottom line is this: there is a winsome world out there, you fill it with your own personal epic adventure. You make it up as you go along. Go and explore. Leave the car where it is. Take a walk.

Like This Feelin' Free

When there's flowers on the palo verde
And springtime stretches west the Rio Grande
Send my friends,
They'll show you where to find me
As I cross this land
When winter's cold
Has crested snow above me
Far below across the plain I spy
Make this soul into a song that's singin',
With wings that could fly
To that snowy mountain perch
Down to broad valleys below
To bring a song of hope
Of trucks and men and rivers that flow
This feelin' I've got to go.

Like a siren's call I hear faintly,
I long to see
Thundershowers brush the desert bloomin'
Like this dry land this thirsty soul it drinks
In all its beauty and God's purpose shinin'
And it makes me think
That I like this feelin' free
I'm like the wind and the rain
Some restless tumbleweed
I'm a trucker's wheels hummin' parade
And I'm rollin' away.

When there's flowers on the palo verde
And springtime stretches west the Rio Grande
Send my friends,
They'll show you where to find me
As I cross this land.
1980

Tinajas, Kielburg Canyon, Galiuro Mountains.

The American Ghost

Morning sun spilling over the ragged edges of the Galiuro Mountains, as the truck trundles up Bingham Ranch road to the gates of Kielburg Canyon and unexpected surprise.

I leave the truck on the high broad shoulders of the canyon's entrance, drop into the boulder-strewn barranca floor, and begin wading through rocks that stand about my height.

Stepping into a small rock room, phone-booth sized, with a boulder in front and one on either side, meaning to climb through in my procession up the canyon. I open my eyes from a blink, to find a long fur train of tendon and muscle drifting past my field of vision. Time passes before my brain can figure out what my eyes are seeing.

Its a lion! My heart pounding with the rush and realization, as it lands on a boulder, inches from my eyes and is gone. I leap over the rocks as the lion did, to see big furry paws and powerful legs bounding over rubble, a long tail trailing into brush a short distance ahead. In hot pursuit, even though the country is open, it is not to be found.

Almost twenty years wandering Arizona back country, I never saw a lion. Their signs are everywhere. The American Ghost. With this sudden apparition, a very exciting five seconds.

Revelation in its size and silence. The giant cat never made a sound, not scrambling out from under my feet, flying through the air, or dashing away. Imagine, deer quietly grazing never know it's coming. There is a moment of being startled, as I was and it's over. Fortunately for me, the lion just wanted to get away. Had he not made his move the moment he did, we would have occupied the same space at the same time. Warning; a rock-cage tangle with a cougar is not recommended.

Just beyond where I can't find the lion, a dry waterfall has been carved from gigantic blocks of rhyolite and obsidian, chiseling a cistern of standing green water and a desperate oasis. In the hun-

17

dred-degree temperatures, deer come in for a drink, lions come for dinner.

I climb steep walls, circumnavigating the canyon's box, dropping back in and wandering for miles in a rapturous joy. Not just because of the lion, though my face flushed and adrenaline flows—it is this captivating and peculiar place. Beauty the gravity pulling me onward, through marvelous rock architecture and the deserts strange flora.

Saguaros stand on stark slopes. Handsome oak groves cowering in shaded nooks. Stagnant water pools carved into the canyon's red floor. Cottonwood and willow abiding in the rocky chaos, awash in a blast of brilliant sun. Beyond the stream where the water should be, vines scamper and grasses advance. The pleasing intricacies and primitive aesthetics, engaging canyon walls climb, enlarging my spirit to the scale of this creation.

The land is older than I can imagine and the ghosts of men long gone haunt these rocky recesses. A good distance up the canyon, a grotto, where pictographs of lizards and deer record some history. An ancient corncob on the cave's floor, an extraordinary find.

More miles and the canyon climbs and the oaks swell over the rising hills. Though the desert retreats reluctantly, on hot sunny slopes only a few trees stand up to the challenge in a blaze of gold grass. The clarion air and radiant sun, the wilderness quickened in the dazzle.

Eventually the canyon closes into an exalted gulf of stone, which harbors a shaded stand of mature maple trees. Bear scat on the grove's leafy floor. Maples on the desert's edge? . . . I'm as excited about the discovery of these determined trees as I am the mountain lion. There are more secrets in these mountains than men could know.

It is very hot and I've come a good distance. My retreat through the canyon unfolds like a dream, a near swoon in the stifling heat and celestial light, where the world shimmers like a mirage on hot macadam.

The life and death struggles are rarely seen. Wilderness days unfold in a calm and peaceful manner, and it often seems that nothing happens here at all. Halfway home, I discover a lion-kill beside a water pool canopied of stately oaks, where ravens scavenge the last of the flesh from the last of the bones. A lot does happen here, but it happens in short bursts.

The day is long and the miles as well. I hobble over the last ridge and peer into the box where I saw the lion. A diamondback rattles a warning.

A three-quarter moon pops over the Galiuro's sharp edge, like the sun just hours before. The truck trundles down the road for home, leaving mountains to moon glow, lions, and the ghosts of men to wander.

Day in Day Out

Day in day out . . . I love what love's about
These mountains . . . these streams. . . .
The songs they sing
The dreams I dream. . . .
Day in day out . . . day in
Day in day out . . . I love what love's about
Mother Earth . . . Father Sky. . . .
The seasons turn
The years gone by. . . .
Day in day out . . . day in.

Day in day out . . . upon this land
I sense God's purpose
In all he's fashioned. . . . clearly shown
Day in day out I know. . . .
Like a field here I've been planted
Unto a harvest we've been sown.

Day in day out . . . I love what love's about
The rivers turn . . . the stars that shine. . . .
This prairie green
Your unseen hand in mine. . . .
Day in day out . . . day in.

Day in day out . . . upon this land
I sense God's purpose
In all he's fashioned . . . clearly shown
Day in day out I know. . . .
Like a field here I've been planted
Unto a harvest we've been sown.

Day in day out . . . I love what love's about
These mountains . . . these streams. . . .
The songs they sing
The dreams I dream. . . .
Day in day out . . . day in
Day in day out . . . day in.
1990

Tumbling waters, Hot Springs Canyon, Galiuro Mountains.

Muleshoe Ranch

The Galiuro Mountains may well be one of southern Arizona's best kept secrets. My hope for the range, that it will remain so. It has earned a special place in my heart, not just for its rugged austere beauty, but more out of a respect for its deceptive topography and this pensive, disconcerting uneasiness that it leaves in my craw.

The mountains have everything but real height and what they lack in stature, other attributes make up for this one shortcoming. Miles of saguaro and creosote line the banks of the San Pedro River, its western boundary. Thick forests of oak choke its rigorous canyons. Higher still Arizona cypress cling to the heights. To the east stretch golden prairies. The spectacular canyon Aravaipa, to the north, a mini Grand Canyon and a national treasure. The Winchester Mountains are a separate range, but somehow attached to the Galiuro's southern end, together form a wide array of flora and fauna, in its diversified terrain of some 1,000 square miles.

One hundred-and-twelve-degree water springs from a hillside in a dry wash of Hot Springs Canyon. Muleshoe Ranch consists of a few buildings, this steaming trickle of hot water and the 50,000 acres that surround it. The Nature Conservancy, an organization that purchases endangered lands, manages there, that the seven perennial streams that flow through these Galiuro canyons and the fish in them might be protected.

I cross the dry wash, up and over a high desert hill, and drop into Bass Canyon. From the crest of the knoll, a distant 7,000-foot escarpment, built with tarnished stripes of tan and maroon rock. The foreground, a jumble of large well-rounded hills, half stone, half grass, like a clump of browned biscuits retrieved from the oven. In the seams between each bun, forests of cottonwood work their way through canyon crevices and present a clear map of the extensive river systems that run through this spacious stone quilt.

In the canyon I stash my pack and walk up the rills for a while. Deliberate and dignified, the crowned jewels of the waterway, cottonwood take an imposing stand stream-side. The bare white bark of Arizona sycamores, stark against a blue sky, their creamed coffee leaves crunch underfoot and clash with the creeks conversation.

After investigating a dilapidated ranch house, a herd of javelina, a side canyon with its adjacent hills, I head down the runnel. My goal for this three-day outing is to walk Hot Springs Canyon, to the San Pedro River, and explore this perennial stream and its environs.

Arizona river-walking is always a rewarding experience. The burden of the vertical climb is gone. Less physically taxed, you're free to drink in your surroundings.

A light breeze moves through stream side jungle thickets. Autumn leaves dance to the rhythms of its measured motion. I strong-arm my way through willow screens. I march through adjacent parks planted in tall grass and stately cottonwood. The canyon cluttered with vegetation, overgrown and gone to seed. Late fall colors the canyon.

One never gets past the novelty of flowing water across a dry land, that this oasis is an apparition and cannot last. To watch and listen to water tumble over a bed of cobblestone is reward enough. But the accord of this landscape's anatomy, the cliffs towering, the bony mountain buttes, the spangling flow of steam, the repose of forest, the undisturbed calm of blue sky, the intricate harmony of this paradise rests heavy on the spirit.

The river flows, and so the miles, and so the afternoon. Saguaros groom the steep grassy hillsides. Cedars tidy the cooler slopes. The last rays of sunlight ride the mountain skylines, and the river bottom grows cold in blue evening shadows.

On a high sandy beach, above the rush of water, under a fluorescent amethystine sky that must be seen to be believed, I make camp. An almost half moon hangs above the ebony silhouette of canyon wall. The white arms of a sycamore canopy the corona of my warming fire. Through the night the swift brook babbles, sometimes speaking in distinct sounding syllables and so much like a human voice, I pause to catch the words of someone speaking, only to realize it is just the whirling water. The stars shine, the waters sing, sleep's the easiest thing I've done all day.

With the morning, frost like a light snow holds everything in its grip. Climbing several hundred feet of a steep hillside, I stand in the warmth of a new days sun; the land reveals itself an extraordinary work of creation. The Catalinas and the Rincon Mountains are blue walls, worlds away. The waters below cut a canyon through the scone brown hills. Chiseled buttes stand watching a difficult land.

The day's course is without the burden of the backpack. The canyon deepens, knifing into its stone floor, thinning the forest to an occasional tree. I walk where the lion walks. At times the whole floor of the canyon is cut from solid stone, where water scoots along the polished surface. But along the sandy shores, lion tracks are everywhere, in such profusion I expect one to leap into view at any moment. Hawks work the skies. Kingfishers chatter. One gray heron appears. Green finches flit through the willows. Turkey vultures fly and float and decorate the day.

The waters twist and turn, low hills rise from the canyon floor, saguaros stare down from the slopes, keeping company with grotesquely bent cedars; stone monoliths rise above these to dwarf the occasional gigantic cottonwood.

Afternoon sun finds me resting along saguaro-studded shores. Cottonwood gold glistening on half-clothed branches. The appease of crystal waters, gurgling.

After logging some miles and with the day wearing down, certain that I am closing in on the San Pedro, I look to climb out of this deepening canyon to gain some perspective. But more miles pass before I can safely scale the now almost perpendicular walls. A way up and out is found, and worth the wait.

Before me is as picturesque a western scene as one might conjure. The stream below snakes its way through a series of retreating blue ridges that plunge to the canyon bottom, forming a gate to the wide and expanding San Pedro River Valley. This sequence of trailing aerial blue cutouts forces the eye to the western mountains, their profiles a never resting ocean waved dyed a deeper blue. Braided silver threads, a river runs. Giant cottonwoods docked along the stream's edge, dwarfed by the swift rising canyon walls, their golden leaves gleaming in the pure rays of a late afternoon sun.

The vermillion rock ridge on which I stand is a desert absolute of cactus and creosote. To the east rise chrome yellow grass hills stacked like loaves of bread to bake in the desert sun.

25

With the golden hills that rise before me and the red rock ridge upon which I stand, and a hundred shades of blue that stretch out before me into the sun, I am part and parcel of a dreamscape to rival any Georgia O'Keeffe canvas.

A great wind starts to blow and the sun sinks toward the horizon. I must retreat up the canyon and make camp before dark; I'll have to hurry. The sun's last rays probe the canyon halls with its lasers, and the wind plays the canyon like a pipe organ.

A blustery cold moonlit night rewards me with two shooting stars.

On the wings of this wind, a storm approaches. With the dawn the once cloudless skies now threaten. Dark brooding clouds spit rain. Cold searching winds probe the layers of my long johns. I hurry up the canyon, to escape impending doom.

After several hours of walking and wading, fighting the raw winds, climbing out of the canyon drift over the last hill, past the Muleshoe Ranch house and the percolating hot springs to my waiting truck.

Through the next two days, the storm deposits forty inches of snow in the high country and temperatures plummet, a timely escape.

Arizona is just a pile of rocks, though it be a beautiful pile of rocks. It cannot be described as a land of promise in the classic sense. It appeals to me on many levels. And if beauty was all that could be found here, that would be enough on which to be content. I remain convinced that there is more to this than meets the eye. That the things placed before us are representative of deeper spiritual realities not always apparent.

If "Nature is the art of God," to quote Thomas Brown, then landscape is saturated with spiritual metaphor. For what artist worth his salt could be satisfied with painting just the natural objects he sees, but in using these things to tell a deeper story.

Is it possible to walk across a desert land and upon discovering a seep or a spring or a flowing river, not be impressed by the resonant spiritual implications of such a phenomenon? Not in the trappings themselves, which are wonderful and remarkable, but in what ethereal substance they represent. This celestial component, the ingredient that satisfies, and keeps me on the saunter.

And so I remain captivated by the intricate tapestry that is Arizona. I am drawn by the sheer weight of its beauty and this tangible, spiritual correspondence, to walk this Gloryland. The aesthetically pleasing and comprehensive sweep of this creation. Its worthless creosote deserts, the symmetry of its forested mountain skylines, its graceful prairies, its shining rivers. The proportionate arrangement of these contrasting parts. The pleasing impression of its size, colors and forms, have come to rest on my mind like a melody . . . with a melody in mind.

Far Trails

There are streams that flow
Through blue spruce forests
Where the lion lay low
Where that creek music plays
And the chirp of the cricket and the songbird
Form a chorusing of praise
That beckon, climb up, climb up, come see. . . .
That beckon, come wander, far and free
Find rest on peaks that stand in stars.

When deserts smell like rain
When cloud banners christen
This sterile stony grease-wood plain
Through the washed atmosphere
Fragrant sun shafts play those water walls
And then rainbows appear
Like angels they've come to set me free. . . .
They beckon, come search out this mystery
Well, I can't explain things I don't know. . . .
But I must go.

Far trails they're a-waitin' on me . . . valleys vast and still
Vistas undreamed of . . . fair-flowered meadows. . . .
Canyon guarded streams. . . . forests enchanted
Filled with magic dreams.

There are streams that flow
Through blue spruce forests where the lion lay low
Where that creek music plays
And the chirp of the cricket and the songbird
Form a chorusing of praise
That beckon, climb up, climb up, come see. . . .
That beckon come wander, far and free
Now I can't explain things I don't know. . . .
But I must go
Far trails.
1989

28

El Rio de San Pedro.

El Rio de San Pedro

The San Pedro River Valley has a history that is considerably longer than man's recorded accounts of his own. People have been coming and going in this extraordinary watershed for a very long time.

About 11,000 years ago, Stone Age Clovis men were busy battling woolly mammoths and a cold unending. As the wintry wet weather retreated and a hotter and drier climate moved across the land, the Cochise Culture arose. Latter still the Hohokom, as generation after generation farmed and irrigated plots along the life-giving river, while hunting deer and antelope. Farther down the line, the Spanish arrived, and history began as we know it. The history we know is wonderful.

The Spanish Conquistador Coronado marched an army down the river in 1540, in search of Cibola and a quick ticket to fortune and fame. The glories of which they dreamed would not be realized. The very ground over which they tread unawares contained the very riches they were looking for and in time would be revealed to others.

Explorer and missionary Father Kino in 1692 walked the river in search of souls and a place to build a church.

The Spanish presidio "Santa Cruz de Terrenate," was built in 1775 along the riverbanks. The brutal Apaches were unrelenting and the outpost was abandoned.

The San Pedro became a Mexican river in 1821, when they won their independence from Spain and an American river with the Gadsden Purchase in 1853.

The 49ers moved along the watercourse, the only dependable water, as they moved toward the Gila River, on the long arduous journey to California gold.

Edward Schieffelin discovered silver in 1877, and the now infamous town of Tombstone became the largest city west of St. Louis and east of San Francisco. The windfall opened the floodgates of progress, bringing the railroads, ranchers, and miners. The conquest of the American West played out like a movie.

The Apache wars, the cattlemen, the settlers, the prospectors, the shoot-outs and gunfights, the stuff of which Western American history is fashioned, unfolded within the valley of the San Pedro. It reads like a dime-store novel. It may be hard to distinguish fact from fiction, the truth from what we've seen on the silver screen or read in books, but it really doesn't matter. The West is a place for dreams, it requires it of all its residents, and all you've ever heard about the West happened right along this watercourse that the Spanish named El Rio de San Pedro.

The Bureau of Land Management has acquired almost forty miles of the river as it flows out of Sonora Mexico, on its 140-mile northward journey through Arizona, and established the San Pedro Riparian National Conservation Area. Any stream that flows year round in Arizona is a big deal. The San Pedro is the largest remaining undammed river in the Southwest and an ecological treasure.

The river valley has been described as the biological equivalent of the Grand Canyon. Apparently, more mammals than in any comparable area on the planet, excluding a tropical Costa Rican rainforest. Birds, 400 varieties of which have been tallied, half of all the species that can be found in the United States, can be seen flying along the river banks, five million migrant birds in a typical spring; 1,400 plants and counting. There are mountain lions, bobcats, javelina, foxes, coatimundi, even a chance of a jaguar now and then. I'm on my way.

The game plan is to walk the river from the international border where it enters Arizona, north to Charleston, about thirty miles. Logistically, just getting there and back will be the hardest part of the trip, not the trek itself. Because of the river's course and the way the roads run, it's easier to thumb my way to the starting point and back home again than try to get back to my truck after the journey's end. The thumb it must be.

The sun poured through my windows bright, like melted butter, as I downed some breakfast and finished stuffing my pack with necessary provisions for the journey. A shot of adrenaline lightened my step, as I drifted through the cool morning air and the town of Patagonia. Three blocks through the quiet hamlet, Harshaw Road starts its way through the Patagonia Mountains and the second car sends me flying toward the San Pedro some forty miles distant.

Three rides transport me across the wide and expansive San Rafael Valley, almost effortlessly, a near miracle. This quintessential cattle and horse country is as big as it is beautiful and the roads infrequently traveled. A gigantic golden prairie, encircled by stunning blue mountains, where pronghorn antelope stand watching between rides.

With the third ride, I reach the crest of a pass in the southern end in the Huachuca Mountains, which partition the valleys of the San Rafael and the San Pedro. From this high vantage point, I can peer deep into Mexico, can see clearly the San Pedro's graceful course as it slides out of Sonora and starts its long Arizona run, a green serpentine line of giant cottonwood. There is a forest fire burning on one of the Mexican Sierras just across the line and smoke is pouring off its slopes, like a dragster on a quarter-mile run, sending ash plumes for miles through the otherwise clear atmosphere.

The car practically falls off the slopes of near perpendicular walls, as we plunge down the other side of the pass, working our way off the mountain. The road straightens out and a broad grass valley holds sway again.

This is my stop. My ride heads north. I have a four-mile walk southeast to the river. Gale-force winds are whipping across the prairie of gold grass and mesquite, and the burning mountain works like a signal-flare, as I hone in on the green line of river.

About a mile and a half from the river, I reach the international border. A six-foot steel wire fence divides the third world from the promised land. Take advantage of the patrol road that runs its length and dart down the cleared path for the approaching oasis.

I stop my feet, miss stepping on a huge snake. It's not threatening, though I've never seen one like it. Ivory and copper blotched, as long as my six-foot frame, with a fist-sized girth. After a few moments of a kind of stand off, we go our separate ways.

The keen winds are stoking the raging wild fire, so the Mexican mountains flame like volcanoes. It looks like the last days of Pompei as I slide down the final ridge to the river.

Cottonwoods tower and sing with the wind. Water barely flows across the soft gooey sand packed with tiny minnows. The green grassy shores of the stream fall on the retina with surprise and delight. Sand-snipes strain to be heard above the rush of air through the trees. Relax for a few moments and drink it all in. Peer down the watercourse with anticipation. Glory in my circumstance.

Water flows in shallow veins across the stream floor. As I walk along, snipes run just ahead to announce my presence on the river. The banks of the stream are low and beyond the cottonwood margins; the Huachuca and Mule Mountains can be seen protecting the valley's perimeters. Inescapable the bold bright sun; the landscape awash under its intense beams, reveals the San Pedro's thin flowing necklaces of liquid diamonds.

On a May afternoon like this one, 449 years ago, Coronado is leading an army down this river in search of Cibola. It is the largest exploratory endeavor assembled in the Americas; 250 horse men, 70 foot soldiers, 1,300 Indians, 1,000 horses, 500 pack animals, herds of cattle and sheep. This is serious business. They'll go on to explore Arizona, New Mexico, even Kansas, only to return, stone broke and starving. On a May afternoon like this one, 449 years ago.

To my surprise, after about two miles, the river sinks right into the sand. The watercourse that held such promise dries up completely. After filling up my water jars with the last of it, I walk what seems like mile after mile of a waterless stream. Walking is difficult in the dune-soft sand and not at all fun with the weight of my pack. Growing tired and disappointed, have I come this far, to struggle down a dry stream? A river without water, is hardly a river at all.

The day draws to a close. Climbing up a sandy bank, I pitch the tent and work on freeze-dried sweet and sour pork, swatting mosquitoes between bites. The glory sun sinks behind the Huachucas, leaving the land under a half moon's milky light. I'm very tired, just wanting to lie down and close my eyes.

"A city set upon a hill can not be hid." The Mexican Sierras, brightly blaze through the night, like some grand civilization in apocalyptic collapse.

On an evening like this one, 112 years ago, prospector Edward Schieffelin is looking for some color in the locale hills. Tonight, he's feeling lucky, but he won't spark up a fire for fear of marauding Apaches. On an evening like this one, 112 years ago.

With the morning the world looks better. I break camp and step back into the dry river. A quarter mile, the water springs forth from the desert sands. Back in business.

Indescribable, the appealing allure of the river. A treasure trove of color these early morning hours. The cool shadowy canopy created by the protective cottonwood. Dazzling sunbeams pierce the green-leafed roof and play on the sparkling flow of water, like spotlights on a country singers sequined suit. Striking vivid greens, brilliant against the blue sky. The atmosphere, flawlessly clear, to match the liquid crystal at my feet, pungent with the perfumes of a world boundlessly alive. A living, watery, verdant tunnel, across an ocean of golden grass.

Water flows over a flat bed of soft sand perhaps thirty feet wide. Shallow water channels weave their way back and forth across the slightly tilted table as it rolls down long sheltered corridors, built of stately trees. Little tadpoles and minnows in countless numbers are placed into every available drop of water.

I am not a bird watcher. It matters far less to me what they are, but that they are. It's no wonder people come from all across the country to see what flies and funnels through this valley. The obvious vermilion flycatcher. There are green, blue, and yellow finches. There are kingfishers and falcons, Harris hawks and redtails. Egrets and great gray herons lift gracefully off the water with each bend in the river. Brown ducks quack above the trees, while mothers with the broken wing routine, try to divert my attention, as the little ones run for their lives. Snipes or perhaps some kind of plover continually walk in front of me with an unending, peep . . . peep . . . peeping.

It's a lot of fun walking a river like this. The sense of wonder and discovery never dissipates. Each bend has its own temperament. It is with joyous anticipation I peek around each turn to see how it presents itself anew.

On a morning like this one, 1,200 years ago, Hohokom women are irrigating small plots of corn and beans. Men are out hunting for

34

deer in grassy prairies. Children are playing in the water. On a morning like this one, 1,200 years ago.

The San Pedro gains a slight increase in its volume of water. Sometimes it's a babbling brook, or a river fifty feet wide, three and a half feet deep. But more often its languid and sluggish flow, slinks like a snake over a wide sandy bed. Very picturesque and reminds me of Nashammany Creek, a stream I knew well as a boy, back in Pennsylvania; then again, it isn't like that all. Often reminiscent of some color canvas, fashioned by a "Hudson River School Painter," of the eighteen hundreds, on the American wilderness. Stately tall trees reflected in tranquil waters cast a Victorian shadow across a land wild and untamed.

On May 27, 1849, A.B. Clarke, bound for California gold, moved down this section of the San Pedro. With three men in his party, they attacked a grizzly bear. They dropped him three times, but he kept coming. With the bear very near, and with his last load of buckshot, he let it fly into the face of a beast gone ballistic. They all ran, the bear in one direction, the men in the other. That was the last they saw of him. The river is not so wild these days, but it's a comfort to know that lions still prowl these sheltered shores.

The river is mine alone. I can climb the banks and see ranches in the distance and there are at times fields quite close, but on the whole, the river seems left unto itself and me with it.

The day is a series of enchanted landscape paintings. I strain to make mental notes on each bend of the river, hoping to remember it all, an impossible task.

Turn after turn and stretch after stretch, the river flows, mile after mile, the powder-dry shores don't drink it dry. I keep expecting this to happen. It has not rained one inch on this valley in four months. The sun, every day, unrelenting, beats down on this valley. How does the river proceed?

The real question is, will this endangered river keep trickling in the years to come? Sadly, 90 percent of the free-flowing streams in southern Arizona have disappeared, due to man's exploitation of the ground water, killing the living waters and taking with it all the extraordinary life dependent on it. Sierra Vista, a small but fast growing city on the shoulders of this valley, threatens to do the same here. I pray that won't ever happen, for that, my good friend, would be nothing short of sin.

Great dry tributaries enter the San Pedro at different intervals. Having run for miles across the broad valley, they give up their bounty to the river's increase. Though these big washes are dry as a bone at the moment, when running, they have the potential to magnify the waters flow to alarming proportion.

Once I met a man, who with his family, was picnicking on the San Pedro some forty miles downstream. A great flash flood came upon them. A mad rushing wave of water, with trees being turned end over end, raced down the river. Scrambling up the river walls, they escaped just in time with their lives. Such dangers do not exist for me today and it's hard to believe that they ever could, as I wander mile after mile down this placid and peaceful stream.

I startle some resting deer in a thicket of cottonwood and like an exploding grenade, they fly in all directions. Though one lingers, perhaps to see if I might give chase, I assure him that can't happen carrying this weighty pack. Not being completely convinced, with two bounding leaps he's gone.

On a morning like this one, 129 years ago, Cochise and a raiding party of twenty are returning with some stolen horses from Sonora. They will stop for a drink here, before bolting across the desert and disappear into their Dragoon Mountain stronghold. On a morning like this one, 129 years ago.

Big frogs jump and plop in the water at my approach, but they're so fast I never see them. But not in any number to match the prolific quantity of tadpoles in the water, which without exaggeration must rank in the billions. A discovery is made.

Resting on a grassy bank, watching the water flow, I come to realize I'm not alone. Suddenly the very ground on which I sit is alive with tiny little toads, the size of my thumbnail. In unfathomable numbers, like a locust plague, the ground writhes in frolicking frog-flesh. It is nothing short of fantastic. I assume the healthy population of herons must be gorging themselves on these miniature amphibians. If you're a lover of frog's legs, it's a glutton's delight.

The river is a beguiling green serpent, the enticing terrain through which it flows. The majesty of the mountains blue. The valley's sweep of gold grass. The green string of cottonwood pearls, that is the rivers bounty. The accord of these component parts, that form this landscape and the splendor of life upon it, these things attest to God's Glory. Though I am a man like any other, I feel closest to Him on these excursions. Perhaps this walking and my wonder-filled gaze, my best form of worship.

On a glorious day like today, 230 years ago, Father Kino, under a broad-brimmed hat, is moving up the river. He's looking for converts and possible mission sites. He's making a map of the river's course, noting the position of the mountains. He's making friends. On a glorious day like today, 230 years ago.

There are roads that bridge the river. I know the fourth one will be the road that leads me back to civilization. At the close of the day, having passed the third bridge, by a good distance and being very tired; I look for an appropriate campsite for the night. It's been a good day.

Walking up a waterless draw just off the river, I come face to face with a doe resting on a grassy bank. Turning my head for just a moment, as I set down my pack, I look up to find her gone.

The soft sand makes excellent bedding for my tent and I look forward to sleep. But not before the distant Huachucas are painted lavender and vermilion ribbons of smoke from the still flaming Mexican forest fire, flag against a burnished copper sky and the sun calls it another day.

On an evening like this one, though probably colder, 11,000 years ago. Stone Age Clovis men have killed a mastodon, on the hills that rise up before me. There is celebration and good eating. The bones and stone projectiles that they have used to slay the unreasoning brute, will be found by modern man, on these very hills. On an evening like this one, 11,000 years ago.

Morning temperatures are cold and after breakfast, I scrape off the ice from my formally soggy sneakers and step back into the river. With the first three steps, a great blue heron lifts off the water, the curtain rises, and the show begins again.

37

The headliners are the ducks. Sometimes bursting off the water in groups of fifteen, but more often, in coveys of four or five and winging over the cottonwood with surprising speed. Lots of herons and egrets, a very large black snake, and a cameo appearance of a strange and extraordinary hawk, the likes of which I have never seen. Six javelina. One kit fox. Three coyotes.

It is a handsome river and each turn proves it. The morning unfolds like the day before, one lovely stretch after another, the river unwinds.

I've dropped in elevation since the river's start and the grass-land has given way to creosote. After a few miles, low desert hills move in close and it is apparent there's a harsh reality beyond this green oasis.

I pray this paradise goes on forever. But another world, regret-fully, does exist beyond this river. After a morning march of five miles, I arrive at the fourth bridge and the ghost town of Charleston.

On a morning like this one, a hundred years ago, wagonloads of silver ore are coming down from the hills of Tombstone, for pro-cessing mills along the river. Charleston is one swingin' commu-nity. It goes on all night long. There is a continuous flux of miners, prospectors, gamblers, ladies of the night, and of course occasional gunfights. Doc Holliday and Wyatt Earp are sleeping in. On a morning like this one. One hundred years ago.

The San Pedro River will run another hundred miles north, emptying its waters into the Gila, and in turn the Colorado, and then on to the Gulf of California. Though these days except for floods, the desert sands drink the waters dry a handful of miles ahead. The river remains government protected for as many miles, but it's closed to the public. This as far as I go, twelve noon.

Just off a quiet country bridge, I stick out my thumb. Three rides transport me back to Patagonia, and by 2:00 P.M. I'm sitting on the porch of my humble abode. I cannot be sure that I have not just awakened from a dream, or that all this has not actually all gone down as stated. Though my soggy shoes and muddy pants attest clear evidence that an engaging ancient river still runs down a grand sweep of valley, and I trust will continue to do so, for the next ten thousand years.

To speak of sparing anything because it is beautiful is to waste one's breath and incur ridicule in the bargain.

John C. Van Dyke

The San Pedro River and this valley are remarkable. The Nature Conservancy, when looking around the country and assessing ecosystems worthy of protection, put this valley in the top five.

Along its journey from here to the Gila River, there are a few places where water springs from the desert sands and flows for a few miles along the surface. The resulting oasis is nothing short of magic. There is a segment along Cascabel, another east of San Manuel, and a good segment north of Winkelman.

In the years to come, I will buy a home in San Manuel and will spend a near decade wandering every tributary canyon, every mountain range that rings the valley. Logging hundreds of river miles, walking its verdant course and exploring the exceptional deserts that border this singularly stunning stream. I consider these places my own personal property.

Just the Galiuro Mountains east of San Manuel is a block of wilderness worthy of National Monument status, but of course this is the last thing I would propose for such a wonderful place. But it is not hyperbole to say, it is only a measure as to how much I think these natural resources are worth. The seven perennial streams that contribute to the San Pedro's watershed and of course the glory of Aravaipa Canyon.

Buehman Creek, the only living stream on the eastern face of the Santa Catalina Mountains and entering the San Pedro in the same general area, has been a source of spiritual and photographic inspiration for years. Some of those images I share with you in this book.

One of the luxuries of residing here is that I live in a huge, empty unpeopled valley, with abandoned bountiful blocks of wilderness. Even if you don't go in, it's nice to know it's there. Isn't that why we have all moved to the Southwest? It can't be just because it's sunny. It is these large open spaces, which set our souls free and our hearts to flutter. But a desert is just a desert until you find a magical stream flowing across it.

We have all come from somewhere else to fill the Arizona wilderness with an ugly city. If we drink these waters dry and kill the very thing we have come here to love, we will have shown ourselves very poor stewards.

Ecological issues, for me, are a crashing bore and like theology, no one can agree on anything. This incessant bickering leaves me weary in spirit. It makes me want to throw up my hands and take a walk somewhere. If there was ever a place worthy of our concern and protection, it is these tributary streams and this beautiful river.

Hilltops High and Fair

It is well to live in the valley sweet
Where the work of the world is done
Where the reapers sing in the fields of wheat
As they toil beneath the setting sun
But beyond these meadows the hills I see
Where the noise and the traffic cease
And I follow a voice that calleth to me
From the hilltop regions of peace.

There are mountains that wait. . . .
Beyond these city gates
To the hilltops high and fair.

To live is sweet in the valley fair
And to toil beneath the setting sun
But my spirit yearns for the hilltops air
When the day and its work are done
For a presence breathes o'er those silent hills
And its sweetness is living yet
The same deep calm all the hillsides fill
As breathed over Olivet

There are mountains that wait. . . .
Beyond these city gates
To the hilltops high and fair.

And there God's finest whispers to hear
In bright streams running clear
On those hilltops high and fair
It is well to live in the valley sweet
Where the work of the world is done.
1995

The Grassy Ridge, Galiuro Wilderness.

The Grassy Ridge

The Galiuro Mountains are the scenic backdrop from my residence in San Manuel. From my windows an unending color show holds my attention and continues to deepen my appreciation for this range set apart.

In the blue shadows of morning, the Sierra is a cardboard cut out, a waving line of indigo. Afternoons flood its contours with light and define them for what they are, a bad-ass crumple of rocky ridges, struggling to support a forest oak and pinion pine on its heightened crowns. At its feet a flowing apron of stony slopes, filled with saguaros and creosote that collar the mountains, forming a wide waterless protective perimeter.

They can leap from the ground like Everest when cumulus troop. On cloudless days when washed of color, they're small in stature, velvetized and dreamy in a storm. With the glory fires of evening, molten canyons anvil out the final shapes of another magnificent day. Sunset mountaintops glow fluorescent lavender under a desert moon.

Dr. Hendrickson owns the ranch and works the range below the Grassy Ridge. He is kind enough to unlock a ranch road gate, letting me gain access to YLE canyon and unexplored territory.

I leave the ranch house behind, the road winding through several small canyons, climbing the gradual slopes choked with cactus, creosote, and occasional cows. Not far from a stock tank and windmill, park the truck and I'm on my way.

YLE starts out with a wide rocky floor and low rising saguaro-filled hills, the imposing blue wall of the Galiuros three miles distant. Sunny and warm, though clouds are building as I press through a jungle of mesquite and thorny brush near impenetrable. I bob and weave, but can't escape the clawing at my pack and the tearing of pant legs as I labor over cobblestones.

A small mountain runs parallel to the main ridge, creating a small valley from which YLE drains. I make a sharp right and move up the draw; saguaros give way to oak and open grassy slopes.

There is a raw edge to the look of these mountains that is unnerving, uncultivated, and unkempt. The landscape looks like a scene from a Hobbit novel, should some goblin leap from the bush. Gnarled, dwarfed oaks no bigger than men, crouching in the corners. A lingering loneliness about the place, and yet contradictorily beautiful. In several places, water springs from the ground and the stream runs for a while on the surface, extravagant rugs of grass and flower. Deer grazing green lawns beneath the trees. Sun playing the field.

By the time I've logged a few miles, the clouds have turned to thunderhead and brought a light rain, as the little valley ends where the small mountain hitches onto the big one. A sharp left turn and two thousand feet up the Grassy Ridge.

Rain ends with a sunshower as I stand on a grass and mesquite terrace above the drainage. Brilliant sun, silver sheets of rain, deer running for their lives.

I advance with the lumbering pace of a deep sea diver; the afternoon is moving faster than I am. This rough and tumble landscape is straight up and down. Cool stiff winds racing up the ridge. It's partly sunny, but I'm often beneath cloud shadows. I'm sweaty, chilled, and working hard. My heart pounds like a locomotive and muscles strain against slopes unforgiving. I believe I can muster the physical strength to climb these mountains, but this stifling topography extinguishes the will.

The trail barely discernible as it zigzags over rocky ledges, then a steep spiraling stair, as I follow above a drainage that is carving a deep seam in the mountainside. Upward to a small landing, the trail disappears completely. I can't tell where to go, but the only way is up, almost perpendicular now.

There is nothing but gold grass and the wind. Higher still, to a shelf where woodlands of pine, cedar and oak make a sudden resolute stand against a determined sun. I drop my pack and walk to the edge of the earth.

Kielburg Canyon plunges into an abyss two thousand feet deep, a narrow defile separating the Grassy Ridge and the massive stone burg, Kielberg Peak. In its shadowed facets, a forest of cypress, clinging to slopes that free fall from seven thousand feet.

The trail leads up a mild incline to a wooded saddle. Then the final six hundred foot assault. The trail is not clear, but it's uphill from here. A dense forest of stunted oak, not much bigger than myself, clutters the swelling hillsides. I puzzle over the trail, pushing my way to the top of the mountain, reaching a golden grass plateau with well-spaced alligator juniper trees. Walk to the opposite edge of the mesa for a marvelous view.

Loosely defined the Galiuros are two great parallel rifts; having reached the top of the first, a panorama of mountain ridge and valley unfurls. A blue wall, of seven thousand foot peaks, tumbles into Rattlesnake, a gigantic canyon draining half the range. Forests of Douglas fir and Arizona cypress clinging to shaded nooks, working down the drainages. A ridge flowing off my mountain drops into the valley below, partitioning the Kielberg basin, a huge forested bowl that punches through the Galiuro's western walls with a frightening gash. Kielberg Mountain is a blue Gibraltar, cut like crystal, catching the golden sun of evening.

The Galiuro Mountains are derelict of any methodical topography. A countenance of chaos on the Arizona landscape. But there on the Grassy Ridge, the mountains make sense. There is a balance and symmetry to its rugged disorder, one of southern Arizona's best views.

I pitch a tent underneath the outstretched arms of a juniper, five hundred years old if it's a day. Pleasant evening, mild temperatures, a fragrant fire of cedar, a billion stars.

The most comfortable night's sleep I can ever remember in the wilderness. With the morning glorious sunshine, gold grass, blue mountains.

I don't know where I'm going, so before I break camp, I do some exploring. The Grassy Ridge is a wonderful formation, shaped like a loaf of bread, steep sided, rounded flat top. The southern end, where it tumbles into Kielberg, is broad and wide, but the ridge as it travels north, tapers at first slowly, then pinches into a narrow wooded blade. To the west it drops off precipitously, twenty-five hundred feet to the desert floor. The top of the table is slightly tilted to the east and at its edges drops off sharply, but more flowingly into forested canyons.

One aspen tree growing just below the western lip of the plateau, on a small talused slope, standing in the shade amidst a forest

45

of pinion pine. You have to walk this land to appreciate its nuance. There are not one hundred aspens growing on this whole mountain range and none on western walls. This is the last tree, in a stand of trees, grown here for ten thousand years. A sapling, growing up beside it, had not survived. Perhaps too hot and dry now for this tree, even to reproduce. It is the last of the Mohicans and a thousand generations.

Centuries long past, Douglas fir filled this plateau and groves of aspen gloried in unseen autumns. Over time, the sun chased the trees into the shadows and aspens to disappear completely, except for one. Perhaps this Sonoran sun will retreat and cooler seasons return, and with them the former woodlands. I'm betting that won't happen and witness the end of an age.

I find the trail I'm looking for, walk back across the plateau, break camp and down I go.

A streamer of trees flows off the Grassy Ridge, declining into the central canyons and a clear trail leads the way. I drop a thousand feet, with glimpses into Rattlesnake Canyon and unobstructed views into the font of Kielberg, as the Grassy Ridge rises behind me, more like a leavened loaf.

At the bottom of the wrinkle, I park my pack. I drop off the saddle into Kielberg, to visit Powers Mine, then into the depths of the bowl.

The small valley is a hallowed pocket, where stands of ancient cypress cast a primeval spell. At the headwaters, a quiet brook tumbles through a deepening ravine, to carve a wedge between Kielberg Mountain and the Grassy Ridge and a colossal canyon. I don't know just how far this barranca can be traversed, but one thing is for certain, no one ever goes down there, not ever. Back up the saddle to my pack and lunch.

In 1915 the Powers family began working on a claim on the ridge just below me. They had gumption and enterprise, building a road twenty miles from the tiny town of Klondike, through lonesome Rattlesnake Canyon, up and over this ridge where I sit.

They brought in heavy equipment to work the mines and ore crushers farther down the canyon and built a house called Powers Garden. Capital layout had to be substantial. I have little faith that they could have gleaned enough treasure to make it worth their while or mustered the strength to accomplish the building of a dream, which in the end brought tragedy.

The Powers weren't winning any popularity contests back in Klondike. When the Powers boys didn't volunteer to fight the war to end all wars, they sent out a posse. After the gunfight a sheriff and two deputies were dead, as well as Powers Senior, and Arizona's largest man hunt was set in motion.

Their crime was self-defense. The authorities came in shooting, the Powers shot back. Though the truth will never be known, the brothers spent most of the rest of their lives in jail.

After lunch I march down the switch-back road that Powers built and drop into Rattlesnake Canyon. I make camp where the road meets the stream and spend the rest of the afternoon walking toward Powers Garden.

Lots of good water tumbles down the stream's cobblestones and the wide flat canyon floor is filled with handsome ponderosa, skeletal sycamores, and the regal oak. These woodlands are planted like a garden. I marvel to think that with a random throw of seeds, a timber stand could raise itself with such aesthetics. That mile after mile it should go on this way. That this much space could still be untouched.

For diversion, I wander up Corral Canyon heading east. Very clear tracks in the sand. Lions and bears, oh my! I press on, hoping to get lucky. I run out of gas.

There's no shortage of wild critters wandering these jungles. But try and catch something move, apart from the blue flash of a racketing jay. A herd of elephants could be interspersed in this tangle of trees and remain undetected, though walking long corridors, through stately groves is reward enough. I return to camp an hour before it grows dark. I prepare for a cold night. Deer in the shadows as I gather wood.

Thank God for long-johns and a fire; without such luxuries this explorer would perish. I cuddle the flames like a lover. Beyond the fires glow, its an icebox. My breath a long smoky column. Through a pine canopy's open windows, a billion stars cannot warm the arctic ebony hours. A cold night in a cold bag is in small measure, eternity.

Slow to rise, for the morning is as cold as the night. After breakfast, I head up Rattlesnake for the most beautiful part of the trip.

Rattlesnake Canyon starts its long run by tumbling off the western face of the eastern rift of the Galiuros, then turning to run between the mountain chain's parallel ridges. The canyon gradually climbing up the mountainsides, the walls closing in, being more shaded by topography, where a marvelous Canadian forest resides.

These mountains are filled with curious sequestered niches, where biologic communities have survived by caprice of sun and shadow. What makes them more the magical, higher still, on mountainsides that carry the weight of a summer sun; only stunted cedar and agave can summon an appeal.

Along the cool canyon bottom, old growth stands of gigantic Douglas fir and ponderosa bring a cathedral silence and majesty, with under stories of dead fern and leafless maples, and a handful of aspens that shouldn't be there.

A divine composition of rock wood and water. This walk of a few miles is an act of worship, done with reverence and awe, with a joyful exuberance. If heaven more handsome, we're in for a treat. Though best to visit in summer when bears roam, or fall when these maples set the forest to fire with color, any season, every man a believer. For in such exultant beauty, has not God his hand in?

Humbled by eminence timber, I browse the sylvan galleries, climbing to the head of the canyon and dropping over the top of the ridge where Redfeild starts its run. I peer down the somber gorge, which drains the southern half of this wilderness. Paradoxically, there is a singular melancholy that rests on this land and cuts to the core. Solitary and estranged, a wild and woolly look to the place that leaves my spirit perfectly unsettled. A trail should lead the way, but it's completely overgrown. I turn back for camp, to wander again the garden alone.

Despite the affectionate lights filtering through the canopy, I can still discern a hint of my breath in the lingering cool of this canyon bottom. Another cold night does not appeal. I head for the Grassy Ridge, in hopes of spending the night in a more temperate location.

Under a warm brilliant sun, up the switch back road to the top of the saddle, leaving the ponderosa and Douglas fir, up the blue ramp through thickets of oak and the juniper. A pleasant climb to a waiting plateau that takes most of the afternoon.

I reach the summits, growing more appreciative of this sculpted formation. A retreating sun washing over the tilted grass table, golden waves marching in lockstep with the breezes blowing. Far below Kielburg and Rattlesnake, the eastern Galiurion rift, tumbling blue canyons, startling blue mountains. The great blue outback.

Make camp under the outstretched arms of a welcoming friend, gathering fragrant cedar to warm the night and spend the day's last light taking pictures and staring into the plummeting blue dim depths of Kielburg.

My kingdom for a fire. The black night all stars, very cold. Warm with the morning sun, blinding light, bleached blond fields, the blue dollops are cedars, a blue clarion air.

I make a dash across the plateau, northward along the narrowing roof ridge. From the crest of its wooded blade, the wide desert valley of the San Pedro River is airbrushed a spring green. The long gorge of Rattlesnake, where tall timber strain the rays of the morning sun.

There's crackling in the woods. For a moment I exult in the presence of the bear. He worries over mine, throwing himself off the precipitous mountainside, into a labyrinth of manzanita as tightly woven as my shirt. Gone.

This beleaguered scrub does not strike me as good bear habitat. I'm wrong. Come summer they're busy here, droppings are everywhere.

On the way back, I find an interesting rock that looks almost like opal.

After lunch, I start a slow descent for the desert and home. With measured steps, I lower myself down the falling mountainsides, growing warmer by degrees in elevation. Through the stunted oak and pine. Down the plunging grass slopes to the headwaters of YLE canyon.

On the small mesquite terrace above the drainage where I stood in a gleaming sun shower three days before, I startle a drove of deer. With much snorting and grunting, eight charge up and over a small mountain in minutes, that would take me an hour to climb.

49

An eighty-degree spring day in the desert. Winter rains have produced verdant lawns where deer find good grazing. I saw only four in the high country, but it will soon warm there as well, renewing mountain meadows and summoning these herds to fill the forests with a delicate presence.

There is elation in fatigue and triumph in having gone the distance, with more miles to tread through YLE. Past the Hobbit oak groves and the short runs of flowing stream. Past the green grass rugs, where more deer dart. On through the ocotillo, the cholla, and the prickly pear. Come the saguaros and the brittlebrush blooms and all the desert hillsides. The finale round, wrestling a wilderness of thorny mesquite to my truck.

The always brown desert is green and yellow. Late sun, washing the rocky faces of Sombrero Butte, Rhodes Peak, the Grassy Ridge. The truck climbs through the long canyons, across the broad benches, down the pleated rock aprons to the San Pedro's riverine cottonwood, the Hendrickson Ranch, the end of adventure.

Something happens to the spirit when it tests itself against mountains and revelation at its culmination.

Deeper than canyons, older than mountains, I would that I had wings.

At night before sleep finds me, I fly over desert canyons to a lone aspen on a distant slope. Over blue forested mountains, into the depths of lonesome canyons, to light by streams beneath whispering fir canopies, finding a rest and joy in the work of His hands, and a peace beyond this beauty, deeper than canyons, older than mountains.

I would that I had wings.

Patagonia

Left a girl in Patatgonia
Her pretty eyes I'll wait to see
I've gone down to Mexico
She waits there for me.

Left my dreams in Patagonia
On a ranch in grassy seas
By the trees she kisses deep
And waves good-bye to me.

Through the sun and the rain I'll ride
Search some canyon there and hide
A woman cries and a posse rides
And the townfolks
Choose their sides in Patagonia.

A man could die in Patagonia
In a stupid test of foolish pride
The shot rang out the bullet deep
A man takes off and rides.

Left my dreams in Patagonia
A sweeter love they'll never be
I've gone down to Mexico
She waits there for me in Patagonia
Patagonia. . . . Patagonia.
1979

Temporal Canyon, Santa Rita Mountains.

Exaltation in Temporal Canyon

Dilapidated in spirit, after my crushing defeat in Nashville, and with the anguish and grief born with my realization, that there is no salve or cure, for the open festering wounds of my thwarted song-writing aspirations, Patagonia has if nothing else, been a soothing visual consolation for this wandering minstrel.

Sandwiched between the towering blue pyramid that is the Santa Ritas, and the consecutive oak ridges that form the Patagonia Mountains, sits a small tranquil community, watered by a perennial stream, from whose shores spring voluptuous stands of cottonwood, housing exotic bird populations from all over the southwest and Mexico. It is a place without debate, one of the loveliest in Arizona. A pastoral paradise of endless stretching prairie, forested mountains that birth rivers, which sing across serene and untroubled valleys, where the pronghorn antelope still roam.

Temporal Canyon is a great trench that slides off the back of the precipitous slopes of the 9,400-foot Santa Rita Mountains, forming a dramatic backdrop for our daily affairs. Since my relocation, I have walked the gorge countless times, for their is much to see and enjoy.

An intermittent stream courses through the canyon, seamed with cottonwood, walnut and sycamore. Fish frolic in crystal waters. Along the hills and hollows that form the grassy contours of the valley, oak garnish the open spaces with blotches of green. Deer sport through the unfurling woodlands, bear hide in the conifer trees higher still, and the lion, king of these wild dominions, roams free though unseen.

I've climbed Mount Wrightson, the high peak, many times, it practically being in my own backyard. Once again, I throw on the pack and head up the trail on a three-day mission. This is all familiar territory, one of my favorite places. I won't go into detail here, of the mountain's great beauty, the outstanding forests, the symmetry of its skylines; this embroidered and uncommon landscape of wood and prairie. Suffice to say a land majestic and grand.

Which brings me to the reason for my scribbling. It is not what happened on the way up, but what happened on the way down, that was really quite extraordinary.

The third morning found me camped at the crest of the range. After breakfast and a short stroll, I broke camp and headed down Gardener Trail for home. Snow lingered in small patches in the cool conifer forest. Steep descending paths presented wondrous views of the mountaintops towering stone citadel, as stirring lines of canyon and ridge plummeted to meet the graceful distant prairie far below.

It is with a ginger step one walks at times like these. The benediction of the wilderness, the freedom of these moments, the exhilaration of being there, I drift down the trail, fueled by the customary wonder of it all.

Onward the miles and the morning slide by. Dropping two thousand feet to reach Walker Canyon Trail, I move along the top of a pine-filled basin. Obvious bear sign in these woods and a handsome stream that flowed along one of the seams in the mountain walls, where it was clear they would congregate.

Advancing, the miles unfold and so the late morning and early afternoon. Finally reaching the head of Temporal Gulch, peering from the ridge, my eyes wander down the great furrow as it slides off the mountain. My truck waits for me somewhere at the end of this trench some six miles distant.

I have been walking for hours. The rhythm of the trail, the cadence of my marching feet, my labored breathing, my pounding heart, the weight of my pack, the hot dry air, the beating sun, the pulsating breeze; I am moving with the musical flow of the day. There is a lightness to my step, a buoyancy to my spirit. Though my feet are firmly attached to the earth, I am floating, just above the ground, a cork bobbing along the surface of a stream.

Although physically tired, I'm not totally spent, but the hum of my body engine over the miles has placed me in an almost trance-like, hypnotic reverie. Though this is not an apt description of what I am experiencing, it is with some anticipation that I expect my spirit to leave my body and my flesh, to melt into the surrounding terrain.

Something bizarre is happening to me, of which I could not begin, or hope to articulate. Something quite out of the ordinary is beginning to transpire, something fanciful and transcendental. With no way to describe it, except in stale clichés.

As always in walks like these, there is the exuberant joy, the sadistic pleasure in the pain of the physical march. This intoxication would be described as a runner's high, but something more than this is happening.

My body is like liquid, flowing gently, smoothly gliding. Suddenly, I am one with the universe, part and parcel, one and the same. The universe am I. Waves of rapturous elation are rolling over me. A quiet, still inner frenzy of great excitement and expectation is welling up inside me. I have stepped through some spiritual portal, crossed quite by accident into the twilight zone.

Though nothing is out of place, as I am acquainted with each stone and plant and wild thing in this valley, nothing is the same. Turned inside out, it's a contradiction in terms, but I don't even recognize this familiar place.

There is a certain vision one conjures of heaven, and what its spiritual spheres might be like; the quickness of it all, the clarity of mind, the camaraderie of all God's creation, the unspeakable love and peace, the wondrous glory of it all. The unending edge-of-your-seat excitement that never dissipates. What no eye has seen or mind of man conceived.

I have somehow been led to the Gates of the City. Everything looks like it's been shot through a gauze camera filter. As I perceive, through a mist, this beautiful land. It is perhaps that I am discerning the spiritual atmospheres of the natural things placed before me. There's a conspicuous effervesce to every rock and tree, a celestial animation, an ethereal air. I drift through a dream, more real than sleep provides. I am more awake and alert than I've ever been. I cannot get past this novel conundrum, that although I know where I am, for I know this place well, I don't recognize it.

There is a calm about my person that is exquisite. I notice of course the sounds and the music that the day is making, but note more wonderfully, the space between each sound. My throbbing heart is a pad of melting butter. My body is weightless, I am almost outside it. There is an undeniable sense that something is going to happen.

I hear no angels chorusing, though I fully expect them and strain to catch the notes. Cognizant that I am not alone, I keep looking over my shoulder to see who's walking with me, but there's no one. My heart is close to bursting with this confident giddy expectation that something is going to happen. It is undeniable; something is coming. At any moment the heavens could open. If the Lord speaketh audibly to mortal men, my time is near.

Setting down my pack for one of my many rests along the way, I speak to God in a conversational whisper. For anything louder than these intonations would shatter this blanket of silence and revile me a screaming madman. "Father," I ask, "what is it? . . . What is it, Lord?" Fully expecting a thunderous reply, or a quiet whisper to match my own. There is nothing but a peaceful, churchlike stillness.

My spirit, through this whole march out of Temporal Gulch, is poised and ready at any moment to spring from my body. My jubilant heart so moved by the beauty before me and something far more palpable that I can't put my finger on, has brought me to the edge of tears. I'm on the verge of a good cry, but the source of my weeping is from a joy. A mystical, inexplicable spiritual journey, beyond words. Quite real and wonderful; though not easily defined.

And so I keep walking, and I keep looking over my shoulder.

In one more location that will be catalogued forever into my memory, I sit by crystal water pools teeming with fish. Tall verdant grass pads the margins of a restful stream. Walnut trees canopy its flowing course and the sun streams through the branches and rains on the liquid mirror like a meteor shower. A riotous calm, an exalted tranquillity, a quiet serenity flows within and without and all this, attended by an uncanny presence.

Unaccompanied in the wilderness for three days, but since mid-morning, I have not been walking alone. In a bliss ineffable, there is someone standing just beyond the scope of my peripheral vision, that when I turn to see, I can't quite glimpse . . . but there is someone there. "Lord Jesus," I say in a whisper, "Speak with me, Lord . . . for I am listening. . . . What is it, Lord? . . . What is it, Father?" But the sanctuary remains silent. I am not losing my mind and I am completely convinced that I am not talking to myself.

And so I keep walking, and I keep looking over my shoulder.

At about 5:00 P.M., I reach the truck, somewhat reluctantly. Since early morning I have dropped 5,000 vertical feet and marched some twelve to fourteen miles, not an impossible accomplishment in and of itself. But the last six miles of the journey was through some spiritual tunnel. A place out of space and not in time, another dimension, another realm, an inscrutable world, tangible and real, though not corporeal or elemental, as is germane to this one. Look . . . there's the sign post up ahead!

> Now faith is the assurance of things hoped for, the conviction of things not seen. By faith we understand, that the world was created by the word of God, so that what is seen was made out of things which do not appear.
> For whoever would draw near to God must believe that he exists and that he rewards those who seek him.
> *Hebrews 11:1–6*

Disappointed, that the Lord has not spoken in some audible fashion. Yet my faith is not the slightest bit shaken. And so, with a perfect conviction, being fully persuaded that he just might, I linger by the truck a few extra moments, hoping he'll change his mind.

I've Got a Girl in Mind

I've got a girl in mind. . . .
Down south Sonoita way
Where green prairies roll perfect
And hold blue mountains at bay
I've got a girl in mind. . . .
She waits for me this day
On a bend in Temporal Canyon
'Neath Sierra Madre
And there on that farm. . . .
There in her arms
I'll melt like winter snow
Past our doors
That fell on high slopes
Of emerald forests of oak
And raced to bless this valley below
I've got a girl. . . . I've got a girl in mind.

I've got a girl in mind. . . .
And at the close of the day
On the road I'm wired and weary
With emotions all frayed
I close my eyes to see. . . .
That star-filled canopy
And that canyon and our cabin. . . .
On the porch swing we'd be
With the dawn. . . .
With the rain showers on
Clouds blazing like the Fourth of July
And that's how love can be. . . .
As she makes love to me
I haven't wings but no doubt I can fly
I've got a girl. . . . I've got a girl in mind.

Yes I feel sorry for those. . . .
Trapped there in the cities. . . .
With the lives they chose
They could be happy I guess. . . .
But that's not happiness.

I've got a girl in mind. . . .
Down south Sonoita way
Where green prairies roll perfect
And hold blue mountains at bay
I've got a girl in mind. . . .
She waits for me this day
On a bend in Temporal Canyon
'Neath Sierra Madre
And on that farm there in her arms
I'll melt like winter snow
Past our doors
That fell on high slopes
Of emerald forests of oak
And raced to bless this valley below
I've got a girl. . . . I've got a girl in mind.

I've got a girl in mind.
1990

Red Mountain, east of Patagonia.

Red Mountain Bear

June is pouring on the heat. The mercury climbs past the century mark. Santa Cruz County winces under the weight of a summer sun. Just one more day in an endless string of sunny days, hot and dry. The range and woodlands are a tinderbox, waiting for summer monsoons. Without any real rain in the last six months, it seems all of nature should dry up and blow away before that blessed day arrives.

I'm bored. I'll climb up Red Mountain for the sixth time, up to the fire lookout, for lack of something better to do.

Red Mountain is an appropriately named 6,000-foot peak. It is the first in a series of oak and pinioned pine ridges that slide in a southeasterly direction from the town of Patagonia, crossing the line into Sonora Mexico. It's the home of the mountain lion, the coatimundi, of deer and bear, but you can count yourself lucky, should you catch a glimpse of anything that moves through its thick brushy jungles.

It is with reluctance that I walk in these mountains; it seems that there's nothing moving in them. They are not very high, barely pine topped, with no springs, or standing water.

Halfway up the steep slopes of a ravine, I take a rest. I have been struggling through unforgiving thickets of bone-dry stunted oak trees, whose half-clothed branches reach up through the air like arthritic hands praying for rain. What little soil there is exists as powder. The loose stones under my feet, like ball-bearings, have caused me to fall repeatedly like a drunken sailor. With the high temperatures, sweat pours off my brow, stinging the eye. My shirt is ringing wet. Climbing a 2,000-foot slope, in this kind of heat is taxing.

Ten turkey vultures are circling just above my head, floating on the wind as it races up the sharp ridge. I can hear the air, as it works through black feathers. They're scouring canyon walls for a meal, and with this many eyes in the sky, they haven't missed a thing. Though from my vantage point, it's easy to miss things that are placed right in front of me, but today I get lucky.

As I stand up, I look down the opposite side of the ravine. A big bear the color of cinnamon, a perfect match for the rust rock walls, is strolling casually down the canyon just below me. For just a moment, between trees, catch a glimpse, the brush is so thick I lose him and he will not be seen again.

Had I not stood up at that moment, he would have traversed the canyon, his presence undetected. The way this gorge is constructed, its walls closing in toward the upper peaks, and the direction the bear was traveling, he would have seen me coming. I have been stumbling and crashing through crisp brittle branches, making a heck of a racket. Yet he walked down a slope just across from me, quite close, silently stepping across the crunchy ground. I never saw him until he was past and below me. If there were twenty bear in this immediate area, they would work through these thickets unseen.

I picture bear habitat as lush green conifer forests, with floors bedecked in fern and flower, with tumbling clear streams to gladden the day. Bountiful meals distributed through the firs, for wild creatures to gorge themselves.

The Patagonia Mountains are not like this. Though it is a landscape as near perfection, as earthly eyes might hope to see, you could wander many miles over its wooded corduroy and intermittent prairie, to find not a drop to drink. And it appears to me, very few eats available, at least this time of year. It is beyond me that a big bear could live in these dry forests, in temperatures over one hundred degrees and survive.

Climb to the top of the mountain. Talk to the Ranger searching for fires across the rippling blue horizon, then back down. I drink all my water and return to the ranch with a thirst unquenchable. The day's heat has sapped all my strength. Tall fizzing ice-filled glasses, of "The Real Thing" slowly bring me back to a vision of my former self and I think of bears without such luxuries.

Arizona wildlife is abundant but elusive. The signs are everywhere, but try and catch something move. When you're lucky enough to stumble onto something, it's a complete surprise. The bear was discovered two miles from our quiet Patagonian hamlet. Perhaps I should be looking just a little closer to home.

Ocotillo

An intense hot dry desert day
In a typical Southwestern way
Down by the river
That just runs for a day
I saw the mission,
Heard guitars as they played
And it took me away
With the sound of the horns
And the songs as they played
It seemed to call me right into the past
I'm a Spaniard as long as it lasts
I wandered in just to hide from the sun
Too hot to walk,
Could barely stand, wouldn't run
I found some shade
And I dropped to the sand
But cut my hand,
On ocotillo . . . ocotillo.

High in the canyons
Where tall cactus grow
Where the rain cuts rock,
But it cuts it slow
I wandered aimless
To where God only knows
Far from towns and ranches,
Where nobody ever goes
And all time stood still
With creation flowing
In that silent stillness
Birds broke the quiet
As they flew to the sun
And as the day turned to run
I saw some deer
Come and drink from a stream
I pinched myself,

I thought it might be a dream
They caught my eye
And they darted away
Past ocotillo . . . ocotillo . . . ocotillo.

Now that I'm back east,
My life's a mess
I dream of a girl
With dark hair and long dress
She stands on a hillside
Where the ground stays dry
And look, she's standing by. . . .
Ocotillo . . . ocotillo . . . ocotillo.
1979

Cinder Fields, Pinacate Preserve, Sonora Mexico.

Sierra del Pinacate

There are deserts and then there are deserts. The Pinacate is a 600-square-mile volcanic field in the northwestern corner of Sonora Mexico. If you landed on the moon, you might get some idea of the bizarre landscape that stretches south of the U.S. border to the Sea of Cortes. It is a wasteland of craters, cinder cones, and extinct volcanoes. A large volcanic mountain sparsely decorated with Sonoran Desert plants and animals. An archaeological storehouse relatively untouched by erosion or man.

For thousands of years, Indians have occupied the area. They centered their lives round natural water tanks called Tinajas. Lived unhoused on the open deserts. Made trails from one water hole to the next and down to the Gulf. Their trails remain on the desert floor just as they left them.

I have read and heard so much about this place and for so many years. I've come to see what the Pinacate is all about. To find a trail and walk it. It is with a great deal of respect I come exploring this intimidating desert.

Here is a land that receives three to five inches of rain a year, if it's lucky. Where summer temperatures hover at 118 degrees, a moonscape of rock and sand to rival any barren waste this planet has to offer. To add insult to injury, this is Mexico where even the good roads aren't. No good maps are available for the area. The only one I get tells me to be prepared, the roads are bad. If something goes wrong, it says in big bold letters, "YOU'RE ON YOUR OWN." Bad roads, no water, no people, no help if you get into trouble.

The recorded history there is fascinating. Just to the north runs the Camino del Diablo, the Devil's Highway. Father Kino, who seems to have walked every inch of the southwest, was here as well. He was the first European to make the crossing over to Yuma. This blistering waterless stretch of desert is strangely seductive, notorious, and deadly. With just a few Tinajas in isolated ranges from here to there, for those who attempt a crossing, it's a roll of the dice.

The Spanish Captain De Anza came next with a group of settlers bound for San Francisco. But the 49ers left the legacy. If you want to read some sobering stories, read of those who did and didn't make it. This desert is as serious as it gets.

Geography creates its own destiny. The story there is the same as it's always been. A man cannot live without water. If you cannot find any, you will die. Hundreds did and still do. Today, these deserts are traversed both for legal and illegal reasons. For those who dare in the summer, this desert is prepared and continues to prove an undeniable fact: you will not walk long through its heat and live.

I am approaching 200 road miles from Tucson. Mexican Route 2 trails west across a land of sand and toothy mountain ranges. To the south I can see the familiar profile of the Pinacate and the massive lava flows that stretch across the plain like an ugly scab on a healing wound. I turn south, on the only path that gains me access into the area, a road that is basically running north to south, parallel to the range perhaps ten miles distant.

The desert floor consists of rolling fields of grayish black cinders, planted with organ pipe, saguaro, ironwood, cholla, and senta cactus. The road works its way along miles of lava flows. These fifteen-foot high rivers of once molten stone push out across these plains like bulldozers, forming extensive plateaus of crumpled rock. The road can't find a way up and over this titanic obstacle, so it works its way along its contours, as I hone in on Crater Elegante.

There are nine giant craters, called "Maar" volcanoes here in the Pinacate. Like impact craters on the moon, they are deep round pock-marks on the landscape. My truck climbs halfway up a steep flat-topped hill, and I sense it's Elegante. Drifting up and over the rise, I peer into a bowl eight hundred feet deep and a mile wide. Directly across this gaping hole, the volcan shield of the Pinacate rises like a maroon Everest in the distance. To the north red volcanic cinder cones from which brown rivers of lava flow from their bases, out across the black floor of the expanding valley to the east. Elephant trees spring from the rocks at my feet, their thick trunks peeling a papery bark, adding an almost tropical look to this Star Trek movie set.

67

I make a loop around the swimming edge of the bowl and drop off its western shoulders to do some exploring. This landscape is completely unexpected, the sheer economy of the place. It is stark and barren and in that lies the charm if there is any, with a beauty stern and unearthly, dissident and bluesy. It is spiritually astringent. Novel and compelling. I am a stranger in a strange land, and a kind of fearfulness undefined is a nag and a taunt, less over this peculiar place and more over these rough and tumble roads and my truck's ability to get through.

A diligent search for words could not define this recoiling, surreal terrain. I'll try to find a few to describe how I feel on the inside and the welling up of a million confusing and conflicting emotions.

I arrive in the Pinacate having logged thousands of miles on foot across Arizona, and I have loved every aching moment. With every step I am presented with the paradoxical attraction of wilderness. As an artist I am compelled to move through it, to experience the weight of its beauty, to glory in this creation. Then, in coming back, trying to fashion something out of it.

Walking across wilderness has as much to do with meeting its physical demands and participating with the exterior landscape, as it does dealing with the interior one. In spectacular, empty, and sometimes dangerous lands, you are quick to perceive the bare essentials. I have a lot of experience in this department. I've learned a few lessons.

The secret to life, is love and use. The fact that I have not been able to translate my love and this humble gift of song into a practical useful item, not just for myself, but for others as well, has left a hole in my heart so big, you could drive a truck through. The catch is, it actually can't be done. But spending too much time in these resplendent outbacks over time becomes selfish and self-serving, if this can't be accomplished. Jesus was tempted in the wilderness, but he also came back and got some work done. I need to do the same.

For God is a perfect man and found among men. Apart from the rune charm that is the wilderness, there is nothing there but something very beautiful. If in the end you can't share it with someone, photograph it, write about it, or fashion a song, is it anything at all? As a man I too must dwell among men. Yet when I return to the city and see the mess men make, with the streets and the traffic, the incessant building, the shroud of dirty air that hangs like a halo above its confusion, I am left cold as a stone. I want to run back to the unkempt places, only to discover again, I don't belong here either.

Having logged so much time in these wild places, have I grown weary of them? Has a maturity of years brought me beyond these things? Apart from loving these places with my whole heart, is there anything I can do about it? It melts down to the big questions. Who am I? Where am I going?

For the immediate future, it's south, about twelve miles, to find a side road westward leading, that will take me to the bases of the high peaks of the Pinacate. The cinder trail moves out across the valley turning into caliche washboard road so rough that I fear the vibrations will reduce my truck into a collection of unbolted steel parts. What worries me more, there are long runs of soft sand that scare me to death. I've been caught my share of times, it's always alone, it isn't ever fun. My stomach is tied in knots, bound to have ulcers before this day is through. Will this truck make it? Will I escape with my life?

I've never had the kind of money to afford a four-wheel drive vehicle; it is times like these when I bemoan my financial status. This trusty truck has taken me into some wonderful and hair-raising locations. It can and can't do several things. It will walk comfortably over bad roads of hard rock and cinder, but this soft sand is a suicide mission. An accident waiting to happen. I can feel it coming. And as always on these excursions, I am by myself. Where's a friend when you need one? I would happily dance across the deserts with a backpack, but driving here leaves me fearful and faint-hearted.

After I pass Sierra Suvuk, a small red rock mountain, by a mile or so, I start looking for a road running west. Finding one, I come across two Mexicans. Their rundown pick-up stacked high with illegally collected firewood. I don't speak Spanish, but they indicate by their waving and gesturing hands that the road I'm looking for is back the way I came. Who am I to argue? But five miles north and my meager map tells me they're wrong. It's too late to do anything about it now, with the sun sinking over the horizon. I find a road heading northwest closer in toward the Pinacate and I follow it for a few miles, but it's not the one I'm looking for. I pull off the road and make camp. Tomorrow's another day.

With distant song dogs baying, a huge orange moon hovers over the eastern mountains. After dinner, under its diffused light, I stroll across the black cinder hills through the blue night like some goblin on the spook. It is deafly quiet, silent as a sepulcher, hushed and still, with a garnet-hued Pinacate brooding in the distance. I find a trail in the eerie moonlight; it's headed south and I wander for miles.

I am at peace and feel a peculiar affinity with the place. Taking rests I lie stretched flat out on the ground and stare at the stars, half expecting to melt into the landscape, or become a cactus, or a rock and join the ranks of the local constituency.

Some things never change. This evening could be a hundred years into the future or three thousand years into the past. How many centuries of silent nights and fiery days have passed since ancient feet have tread the trail? I press on, though it's haggard and haunt, pushing the limits, probing deep into the darkness through the moonlights day. I guess because it beckons, because it frightens me, because it's beautiful, because I can.

Once on a walk in the Growler Valley, a few miles to the north, I spent a lovely day making a twenty-two mile saunter across the desert. After dinner, as I so often do on these excursions, I walked away from my fire-less camp. To stroll through the moonlit night. I hadn't wandered far, yet when I headed back for camp, it could not be found. I was very close, but it could not be located. I kept making loops, little ones and bigger ones, traipsing back and forth in the general area. Not ever being terribly far from my destination. But it took a diligent search of two-and-a-half hours to find that damn tent.

That was the first and only time I've ever been so completely lost so close to home. Tonight I wander miles from the truck and walk right back to it, as though getting lost is not only of little concern, but a complete impossibility.

Breakfast under the blazing cirrus clouds of dawn. With a little more investigative work across the cinder floors, I'm ready to go. It is a unique and fragile land. Just under the cinder surface lies a fine light brown dust. As you walk across its black "Grape-Nut" exterior crunch, you break through, leaving your foot's impression with

70

a brown earth showing. Every footprint, animal track, or off-road tire track, leaves a near permanent scar upon the land, which explains why the prehistoric foot trails the Indians left, are so clearly defined. I feel guilty walking around and making a mess.

Proceeding southward, past Sierra Suvuk. I find a road heading west. Though I can't be certain where I am in this chaos, judging by my scanty chart and local topographic features, at least I'm headed in the right direction. The road, if you can call it that, is bad. But I've made it so far so good. I begin to think more confidently that this old truck of mine, just might push right on through.

Unbeknownst to me, a fact later to be revealed, the road I need takes a sharp right, out of this wash that the road has been using to its advantage, climbs across a lava field, proceeding onward to the still distant Pinacate peaks. But the car width path, on which I ride, is thickly lined with creosote and obscures the turn. I cruise right on by. A fatal mistake.

Just a little farther up the wash, my truck wheels sink deep into the sands. Up a dry creek without a shovel, or almost. My worst fears realized, and my heart sinks as deep as my sunken vehicle. Eyes glance over to the map that sits on the seat beside me and these big bold letters stare back: "YOU'RE ON YOUR OWN." It is 8:30 A.M., as I climb out of the cab and access the situation. Oh, God, please help me! I am in trouble! I am several days walk from the nearest town, completely alone, and in over my head.

The prayers fly, hands dig, wheels spin, digging a deeper grave. I've got one of those funky collapsible military field shovels, but in this situation, it's nearly worthless. You would have to see my predicament to know how impossibly trapped I am. I can't go forward or backward, held fast by this dry quicksand. Buried beyond the differential, chained to a sand prison.

It's amazing, but I keep my cool. No curse words fly. I keep working. The hours pass. I offer up prayers.

With time, using branches, rocks and brush, with a helpful piece of a small sheet of corrugated steel that I find in the desert, the truck climbs forward, out of the wash, and on to its bank. I'm still headed in the wrong direction, but I'm on slightly harder ground. Still far away from getting back on the road I came in on and far from a safe getaway, the fact that I've gotten the truck this far is really nothing short of a miracle. It's 11:30 A.M.

71

The next course of action is to build a road parallel to the wash, about twenty-five yards and to drop back in on the wash and the road at a point where I can safely proceed, escaping to freedom. This takes several more hours of clearing brush, bushes, and chopping down small trees, rolling away big rocks, as well as trimming thick canopies of ironwood branches that hang overhead; 2:30 P.M.

Another pickup drives up the wash. I flag them down, to prevent them from entering the same sand pit quagmire and certain entrapment.

A friendly American couple, they're more than willing to help me in my pickle of a plight. They have a full-fledged shovel. We go to work.

Can't turn the truck around, so I have to drive backwards over the road I have fashioned. Rick, a schoolteacher from the Four Corners area, works the shovel. Laurel, a Tucson teacher, sits in the back of the truck bed for additional weight and traction. I'm a truck drivin' man.

The wheels spin and we dig them out. They spin some more. We dig some more. Suddenly the tires catch and we're on our way. It's a bash and a bump, through a whirlwind of flying branches, brush and clouds of dust. The truck lunges toward deliverance. In an eternity of just a few harrowing moments, the vehicle ends it roller-coaster ride and we drop in on the safety of the wash and freedom. With the settling dust clouds, it is clear my ordeal is over. Hallelujah! Rick slaps me on the back and says "Welcome to Mexico." It's 3:30 P.M.

There is complete and unqualified relief in emancipation and a perfect intimidation, an outright fear, in being caught again. I want to give up, throw in the towel, to leave this place. I can't stop thanking Rick and Laurel for their help.

Rick finds the road off to the right that climbs across the lava fields and onward, to the far-flung Pinacate. He's convinced it's the one we're looking for. "If I'm not back in twenty minutes, come up after me," he says, "if not, good-bye and good luck."

I sit in the wash trying to decide if I'm coming or going. Rick and Laurel do not return. I have come a damn long way to see this place. Fearfully, I follow.

The road is terrible, at best a cow path across the moon's surface. The only thing that could convince me that I'm not truly on our orbiting neighbor are the hanging blue sky and the occasional cloud. Climbing high up the mountain contours, I reach the end of the line, a place called Red Cone. A cleft in the mountainside forming an amphitheater with its odd-looking red rock walls. Planted with a bizarre combination of cactus, a perfect little park and staging area for an assault on the peaks that stand proud above us.

Rick and Laurel are boiling some water for tea. They invite me over for a cup and a chat. We talk about this strange landscape that we find ourselves in. The crude pottery shards they saw on the ground near the "maar" crater MacDougal, yesterday. Because its too late in the day to do any real walking, Rick and I make plans to climb the Pinacate in the morning.

With an hour before dark, I take a short walk, studying the mountain's topography and contemplating the best route up its slopes. From here, it's about a four-mile walk and a 2500-foot climb up a mountain, that might loosely be described as an ice-cream sundae. Great rivers of lava pour off the peaks like chocolate syrup. These magma flows extend over many square miles, creating a physical barrier to be reckoned with. An obstacle course of jumbled crumpled stone that must be climbed over, in, around and through. The soft ice-cream part of this analogy, the peaks above the lava, are great piles of heaped-up loose cinders, that will want to roll out from under our feet like ball bearings, as we scramble up the 60-degree slopes. It should be an interesting climb. This is it. I've made it, thank God. It's going to happen.

Standing in the shadows of the Pinacate, the late sun is flooding the eastern deserts and the expanding valleys far below. Distant ranges are saw-blades gleaming, as I head back to camp for dinner. Watch a full moon rise and spin my prayer-wheels of praise and thanks, to the Good Lord for my timely escape from the desert sands. If Rick and Laurel had not come to my rescue, I would still be down there digging. I can't now, or will I ever, get past my fear of being trapped again.

At 8:00 A.M. Rick and I are on our way. We climb out of the red amphitheater, across a cinder field, and start wading up the lava rivers.

The lava is as hard as iron and sharp as knives. Springing from the sterile rock grow elephant trees. There are pockets in the lava, where a fine light brown clay collects, as well as occasional moisture, on the floor of sunken rooms. Inside grow desert lavender, yellow flowering brittlebrush, blue solanum, and little barrel cactus with bright red needles that look like rubies set in the brownie mix. Planned and planted like an aesthetic Japanese rock garden.

Beyond and above the lava, we scale the cinder slopes. Ocotillo, palo verde, and dense stands of Teddybear cholla, dress the increasingly steepening slopes. We huff and puff, rest and climb, scramble up the almost perpendicular mountain, reaching the top of Carnegie Peak. The ranges second highest.

To our surprise, the mountain's topography is not as anticipated. We assumed that a saddle tied the two highest peaks together. The Pinacate, the one we've come to climb, is a separate cinder pyramid off in the distance. Another whole mountain to climb, and our hearts sink with the realization. The view is spectacular. A million square miles of inhibited desert and the Sea of Cortes mirrors the sky.

We plunge down the slopes, skiing with the lose cinders, almost a free-fall, and reach its base in ten minutes flat. We cross a hollowed-out valley and climb up the Pinacate, which is higher in elevation than Carnegie, but not quite as steep and it seems somehow easier to climb. At the top we sign the registry. Lunch for two.

In 1698 the Jesuit priest, Eusebio Francisco Kino, climbed the Pinacate. The Spanish believed California to be an island. From this, 3,904-foot mountaintop, he hoped to see if Baha California was attached to the continent. But you can't quite tell. From this position northwestward, to the point at which the peninsula meets the mainland, is obscured by 5,000-square miles of desert, a wilderness of tan sand dunes, the size of Connecticut. To the south blue waters trail, and across the waters, Baha floats on the horizon; everything else is desert. I think Kino a god.

Our variant route back to camp is an attempt to avoid the extensive lava flows, but this is impossible. The slopes we chose aren't as steep and the walk seems more leisurely. Less burdened our conversation flows freely. In a land so set apart, I'm grateful for Rick's company. A little after three bells, we arrive back at camp.

To reward himself for a successful mountain climb, Rick wants to head south to Rocky Point for a seafood dinner. He continues to display greater courage than I. I'll settle for just getting off this mountain and home safely. Down the rugged road we go.

On Mexican Route 8, we wave good-bye. Rick and Laurel turn south for dinner and the sea. I turn north for the border and home, convinced I have seen and experienced enough desert landscape to last a lifetime.

An extended stay in the wilderness might be likened unto a draftee's stay in the military. During your tour of duty, you can't wait to get out. Your reluctance to get with the program. The natural dislike to follow orders not your own, the lack of freedom. You long to escape its conformity and its physical demands. You would be more than reluctant to sign up again. Yet with your honorable discharge, you look back on the experience as one of life's most rewarding.

In my mind's eye, I see long sun shafts shot through the clouds that play on the sparkling peaks of a distant sierra. Rolling volcanic gray cinder hillsides planted with nothing but flowering brittlebush. A moon crater named Elegante. Blue ocean waters lapping a hundred-mile stretch of creamy tan sand dunes. Flowering sunken rock gardens in maroon lava flows. Soft sandy brown washes that swallow green pick-up trucks whole.

These and a thousand other images will play in my mind in the weeks and years to come. These experiences, indelibly etched on the impressionable mind, will remain forever like the prehistoric foot trails on the fragile desert pavement of the Pinacate.

Whispers a Song

I sing the songs that I've heard on high
Beyond tall timber where grand glaciers slide
Down granite peaks that carve a sky of blue
Where cumulus incandescent glow
Could cast aspersions on this life we know
Down in the valley
Where the cities grow and breed despair
But up there I'll find
Rest for the spirit and its peace in kind
Alone with the Lord
And the wind whispers a song.

I sing the songs that I've heard far below
On windswept prairies where the pronghorn go
Dry dusty deserts
Where the creosote perfumes the air
I'm an artist drawn to this aesthetic scene
To marvel at the canyons and its color scheme
Palettes of glory
Formed in rock and stream and tree
Come climb these hills and see
The world as finely crafted tapestry
Embroidered rivers on the loom
Worked by hands Divine.

Listen and hear nature sing
Tall mountain turrets like church steeples ring
Call this believer there to wandering
Through splendid hues of stained-glassed skies
Listen, the congregation sings
This host of mountain plant and wild thing
To choir songs of joy and winter's sting
Under the auspices of Heaven's care
Listen, for it leads me there
Listen . . . listen . . . listen.

I sing the songs that I've heard on high
Beyond tall timber where grand glaciers slide
Down granite peaks that carve a sky of blue
For up there I'll find
Rest for the spirit and its peace in kind
Alone with the Lord
And the wind whispers a song
Whispers a song.
1988

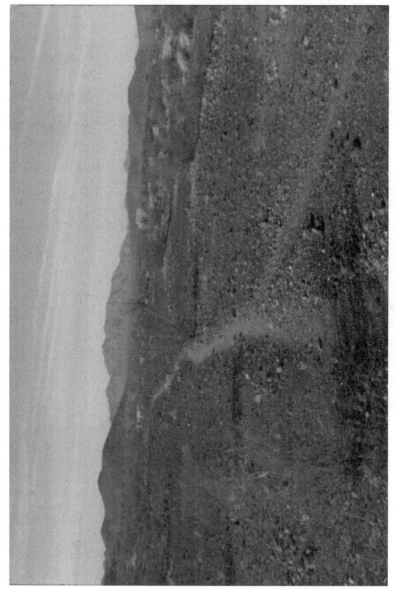

Foot Trails, the Growler Valley.

The Shell Trail

I have been thinking and dreaming for some time, having heard about the pilgrimages that the Indians used to take from the inland deserts of Arizona, down to the Sea of Cortez, a kind of spiritual quest. A walk for shells, for salt, and for knowledge. A trek of hundred of miles, over the worst of what the great Sonoran desert has to offer, which believe me isn't much but a weird and bewitching wasteland.

The ancient ones would walk with what water they could carry, in fragile earthen pots and move from one water hole to the next, eating what they could find along the way and with the knowledge of secret Tinajas in the mountain passes, they moved along the antiquitous footpath to the sea.

I want to do the same as they. To test myself as they did, to walk the paths that this century has forgotten. To taste and to feel, to catch a glimpse of what their world must have been like. Though I can never know, I've come for a visit.

Sunday afternoon stretched bright and beautiful, as well as the road running west across the Tohono O'odham Indian Reservation 120 miles west of Tucson to the mining community of Ajo.

I have everything I'll need for the six-day mission, but a map of where I'm going. I plan to wing it. With just the knowledge of the drive to Rocky Point on the Gulf of California my ultimate destination, and having spent some time in the wilderness of the Pinacate, in northern Sonora Mexico, I hope to be able to feel my way to the ocean.

I'm not totally clear on how to get there. If I fail, I'll crack this one up, as an exploratory mission. If I make it, all the better. I want to walk across a desert that has no end and get a feel for the soul of the place.

From the small town of "Why," just ten miles south of Ajo, where I'll spend the night, I have a hundred waterless miles of desert to reach my goal. I worry not of snakes or scorpions or even

79

the distance, but I'm scared to death of running out of water. I squeezed four gallons into my backpack. I will foolishly carry two additional gallons in hand. Still I worry over water.

Upon reaching "Why," I check at a gas station to see if I might leave my truck there for a week while I journey forth. Get the O.K., and head up to Ajo to check into a motel. I'll get a good night's sleep and set out at dawn.

Dinner at the Palomino, a small Mexican restaurant. The last time I was here, there were guitar players and singers and they were just bad enough to be good. Tonight, I'm practically the only patron, just one other table. The roast-beef special is out of this world, I linger over apple pie and coffee.

The mountains are jet black, sharp-cut silhouettes against the brightening eastern sky, as I head south for "Why." I park my truck, slip into the desert, heading southwest across the valley of the Ajo, my sights set for Growler Pass, a notch on the distant horizon.

The morning air borders on cold and the water I carry in my hands is frigid. In a few minutes, my fingers are throbbing. I maneuver over some barbed-wire fences, an immense desert swallows me whole, disappearing into the creosote, as the sun floods across the serrated ridges of the mountains and fills the valley with an amber light.

This is going to be tough. I am not a beast of burden. The weight of water is going to prove my greatest physical test. But the day is new, I'm ready for just about anything, and with determination, I push across the flats.

The cloudless sky a bright blue blanket. A curious calm hangs in the still air. Nothing is moving but me, no birds, no sound but my breathing and marching feet. Off to my left perhaps ten miles southeast, Montezuma's Head. A towering stone finger in the Ajo Mountains juts into the sky and divides golden sun shafts as they beam their way across the valley floor.

The valley is immense, a swimming ocean of space, ringed by a distant mountainous horizon. On foot, progress against such proportion seems an all but impossible task. But as the early morning hours slide by, I notice that little by little, I'm beginning to make a dent in the endless stretch of flat land.

This place is a wasteland, in every sense of the word. A pink caliche floor and well-spaced creosote bushes, and that's about it.

Washes rush across the open ground, producing green lines of palo verde and iron wood trees. There is not a blade of grass to be found.

I walk a little, rest a little, walk some more and rest again. Climb another barbed wire fence, tear a section out of my pant leg, and struggle on. Far too much water! I'm a fool to carry this much, as it will surely break me. Sometimes I lie prone, stretched flat on the ground, resting ten minutes, then lunge forward for twenty. I drink as much water as I can, just to be rid of it.

Three steer are discovered in a wash thicket and they watch in disbelief as I cross the barren waste. There are not three clumps of grass in this whole valley.

The afternoon stretches out and the Growler Pass nears. By 2:30 the foothills are reached. Saguaros and cholla spring from the rocky ground that is a series of rolling hills that come down from the rocky crags of surrounding peaks. Into the trenches, up and over a small hill, descending into another wash, up and over a larger hill. The clay valleys are replaced by a chaotic rock-strewn unearthly beauty. Fields of rock are sown over the stony acres, as though the mountains had exploded and debris thrown everywhere and anywhere, and where it landed, there it lay.

Reaching the crest of the pass, I climb a mountainside to gain some perspective on my accomplishment and see what obstacles might lie ahead. I've come a good distance, perhaps fourteen miles, though it appears, from horizon to horizon. To traverse such a roadless ocean of space, carrying this much water, seems a task beyond endurance. Pleased with my progress.

The collective greenery of the creosote over the leagues of open space between the mountain ranges, produces an eerie optical effect, as though the mountains are thrusting themselves above green misty clouds or are floating in mid-air.

To the southwest, Growler Pass struggles across the mountain ramparts, a jumble of hills, arroyos, and deep trenches. An obstacle course for this overburdened backpacker.

I've entered the 300,000-acre wilderness of Organ Pipe Cactus National Monument, and those strange plants cling to the bare stone faces of the hills as I struggle over the rough-hewed landscape. The day is quickly drawing to a close, which is fine by me. After ascending and descending one more hill, and exploring an abandoned mine shaft, I enter upon the only road in these here parts. Bates Well is just a mile or so down the road. The only drinkable water for forty miles. That's on tomorrow's itinerary. As the sun sets, I organize a camp, just off the road and work on some dinner.

The sun burned itself into distant valleys and the sky cooled its flaming colors of apricot and carmine to lavender and amethyst, then a sparkling ceiling of stars.

It is December; time for the Jeninid Meteor shower. Lying in my sleeping bag, I watch shooting stars fling themselves across the black night sky. Not one or two, but a continual fireworks display till dawn. So close, with a good catcher's mitt, I could have brought them down from the nearby peaks, to warm my morning coffee.

With the dawn, I pry myself out of the bag. I work on oatmeal, sweet rolls, and coffee, and I finish my first gallon of water. I start down the road for Bates Well.

In 1886 a rancher named Bates sunk a well alongside the Growler Wash and began ranching; he prospected in the nearby hills, and Bates Well earned a spot on the map. Old-timers traveling the Tucson and Yuma Road stopped for water and the news, and the Papagos on their salt pilgrimages, as I am attempting, stopped for a rest on their sojourn. By 1900, Bates Well was a vital crossroad on the Ajo-Sonoyta road, when nearby mines like the "Morning Star" and the "Alice" worked the local hills. In 1927, a man wanted for murder was shot to death by an Ajo sheriff's assistant, as he attempted his capture.

In the dawn's early light, I pass by this small spot of western history, three windmills, two trailers, and one American flag. The road pushes across the rest of Growler Pass and for a mile or two, I use it to my advantage to cross the difficult terrain. Carrying this much water is proving a most burdensome task, nothing short of torture. I can barely hoist it off the ground after a rest, which is too bad, because if not for the weight, this would be the easiest walk I've ever done.

With Growler Pass behind me, I leave the road and skirt the great escarpment of the Growler Mountains. I gaze across a wide and sweeping valley of colossal proportion. Three groups of mountains frame the distant horizon, perhaps twelve to fifteen miles away. The Agua Dulce Mountains are far off to my left; I believe these to be what I call the Lukeville Mountains, with the town of

Lukeville at their base. (I am wrong.) To my right, and worlds away across the valley, the Granite Mountains and southwest the smaller Antelope Hills. Assuming things are as they appear and believe them to be, this should work out as planned. (I am making a fundamental mistake on the positioning of these mountain ranges and will pay for it).

The Growler Mountains are rugged rocky terraces, lifted up like tabletops and from their heightened mesas, debris pours off the fluted slopes, like a flowing skirt of rock. Drainages pour off each grove on the mountain, forming arroyos and washes that race out on to the distant sweep of the broadening valley. Ironwood trees and palo verde cling to the dry rivulets, and appealing pavements of volcanic stone are formed over the rolling hills between each dry water course. I walk for miles along this great rock wall that is the Growlers, negotiating the washes, hills, and thickets of dwarf trees. (I am wasting all my strength and energy, heading almost directly west. Don't ask me why.)

After more miles scale a barbed-wire fence on a north-south axis; I am leaving Monument lands and entering the Cabeza Prieta National Wildlife Refuge: 940,000 acres of rock sand and cactus. Cresting one of the low hills, I look up just in time to see a desert big horn do a quick step into some stunted trees walling a dry wash. A few more miles and I change direction.

I set a course for the Antelope Hills, the middle mountain range on the far horizon, heading south across the valley. Surely the road to Rocky Point runs beyond these ridges. When I find it, I'll know I'm on the right track.

Leaving the Growler foothills, the rocky ground surrenders to the flat creosote valley. Gone the trees and cactus, to a wasteland of creosote, good for nothing but to be crossed and then forgotten.

The creosote bush does have its charm however; it's a survivor. Some of the oldest living things on the planet have been discovered in the California Mojave Desert. Spotted by satellites in space, they are great living rings of creosote, estimated to be 10,000 years old. These larger clumps and circles, though they don't look like much, have been standing in this sun for a very long time.

The afternoon is spent crossing this expanse, with only one memorable thing to note apart from my increasing confusion as to where I am in the grand scheme of things.

Far out into the valley and much later on in the afternoon, I cross the Growler Wash once more. This water course that started perhaps fifteen miles back at Bates Well, has raced far out across this flat expanse and runs perhaps another twenty farther on. It is a serious dry river. I marvel to think that a desert that receives five inches of rain a year, could in a desert downpour, send water racing down from the mountain passes, out across this thirsty clay floor of a measureless valley, without it being drunk dry at its source. Yet as I stand and observe the riverbed, it is clear that water has coursed through its arthritic veins, with the impression of water left in the tumbled sands.

Stately palo verde forests, ancient of days, cling to the powder banks. In a world of nothing but creosote, an oasis of green, minus the water. Birds find a haven in protective branches, and a lone hawk works the empty sky. On either side of this great dry wash, there is nothing but a grease-wood waste.

The rest of the afternoon stretches on. F-14's race back and forth across the horizons. The land is good for nothing, but the skies are good for war games. There are spent shell casings here and there, and I stumble on to two bullet-ridden targets.

At sunset, I rejoice in the day's end, just to emancipate myself from the weight of the pack and lie down. I know what a pardoned prisoner feels, when the door swings open.

The escarpment of the Growlers from this far out in the valley is impressive. A towering blue wall, thirty miles in length, and a lovely shade of lavender air hovers over its stony architecture. The valley floor glows a fluorescent pink, in these sunset moments, as though the ground is electrified. Until the stars take over, the earth has an incandescent life of its own.

Another evening of winging stars across the heavens. These fireballs have become commonplace, as from all directions they race across the glittering star fields. What a show! And through the night, as big a quiet as I ever heard.

At dawn, I savor breakfast and really begin wondering just where I might be. I climb a dead dwarfed mesquite, in hopes of gaining some perspective. With the sun's first rays, I can see some lights beyond the Antelope Hills, which are now quite close. I assume these lights are farms and the road I'm in search of. Along the Agua Dulce Mountains, there are also lights farther to the southeast, where I believe Lukeville should lie. Play it safe, and head for a mark between the two.

No longer being able to abide the weight of water, I obtain some absolution, by pouring a gallon on the ground before I leave camp. At least now I can lift the pack off the ground. One learns from one's mistakes; I've wasted too much precious energy carrying too much weight, with a long, long way to go.

The third day out is one of great physical fatigue, increasing confusion and disorientation. The day's course is a broad southeasterly arc across the base of the mountains that form the southern perimeters of this massive valley. After many miles and the burden of my pack, the lights I had seen in the morning proved to be nothing at all. After many more miles, the town of Lukeville, which I was sure lay at the feet of the Agua Dulce Mountains, proved nothing more than wishful thinking.

Shocked, I turn eastward and set my sights on the southern end of the Cipiano Hills that form the eastern gates of this unending Growler Valley. Surely one of the National Monument roads runs close to these peaks. Perhaps Lukeville is beyond this gate in the valley. If I can climb it, Lukeville can't be far. I'm sure I'll see it from that vantage point.

The sun is making a dash for the horizon as I walk across the backbone of two colossal piles of chocolate-brown volcanic boulders. I am king of the mountain and king of all I survey. But across this endless realm of waste, this measureless dominion of space, I am the only living soul. There are no roads, no lights, no towns, or any indication whatsoever that human beings exist on the planet. If Lukeville endures at all, it is somewhere else and far away. I am not only dumbfounded by the view, but at a total loss, as to where I might be. Fortunately, I am not lost, but I don't know where the hell I am. Having walked from dawn to dusk, I am exhausted, physically in pain, completely befuddled and confused.

But what a view! Words are not to be found that could describe the complete and total desolation of it all. Inadequate my vocabulary, my meager linguistic skill, in attempting to frame its grim glory.

From a mountaintop hundreds of feet above the desert floor, I gaze across this odd uninhabited wilderness and cannot believe my eyes. The great Growler Valley stretches out before me sixty miles in length and perhaps twenty in width. An oceanic valley of creosote looks like the great Australian outback, minus the bizarre plants. As I perceive the distance I've come in the last two days, I want to faint dead away, a gargantuan trackless landscape.

The raw geologic charm of the mountain's rugged ramparts stand proudly protecting the wastes at their feet, while flanking sides pour off the heightened escarpments and fan out on to the flat stark indefinite stretch of the valley, festooned with saguaro, organ pipe, and palo verde. A mighty wilderness, barren and bare, filled with nothing but space and beauty.

I cannot believe that I have come this far, suffered this much pain, and missed my goal by this much. I have come a long way to find that I have missed the mark, big time. Very disappointed with myself. The only course is to return by way of Growler Pass, from whence I came.

I limp down the mountain to my backpack, and do dinner in the twilight, jumping into my bag for the longed-for rest. To lie down is heaven itself. The ebony night reveals three shooting stars. The wind starts to blow for the first time in three days.

It is far too windy to work my stove in the morning light. I forgo breakfast until I can find some kind of wind break, pack up, and start walking. A cloudy sky is welcomed change from the less imaginative blue that I've been witnessing the last few days and it brings out the desert colors vivid and brilliant.

Marching along the bases of volcanic ridges that form the eastern walls of the Growler Valley, I head for Kino Peak and the Growler Wash, for somewhere over there, Bates Well exists, a ranger station and the road to civilization.

Apart from the fact that I am in physical pain, walking with a limp, and want this whole damn thing to end, apart from the fact that my attitude stinks, that I am disappointed with myself, and there is nothing I can do about my mistakes, the day is steeped in a marvelous light and a splendid color is brushed across this bizarre landscape. My mind's eye, like a photographic plate, has captured forever every captivating and desolate scene.

Gale-force winds are whipping the creosote to and fro, and the collective bowing olive branches over the leagues produce a yellowish-green, tempest-tossed sea. The volcanic mountains, the color of fudge, like overdone loaves of bread, collect in the corner of the valley, as sunbeams poke through the cloud holes and reveal possible passes through the strange arrangements of stone.

The early morning hours blow by like the wind. At 10 o'clock, I reach a lovely wash that is snaking its way across the flats as it pours out of the burnt volcanic hills close by. Aged palo verde shelter me from the harsh reality of the creosote waste on either side of its dry shores. In the soft sand, I relax and enjoy breakfast, watching birds flit through the thickets.

With breakfast completed, I bolt across the last few miles of level creosote barrens, before reaching the furrowlike foothills of the Bates Mountains. My rudimentary understanding of geology cannot begin to fathom how such stone sculpture could be fashioned. The odd turrets of rock on the mountaintops. How the desert pavements were spread out at their feet, or the time it took to create such wonders is beyond my reckoning.

It is for sure, this was once a land of fire. From the depths of a fiery underworld, God knows how long this landscape was flowing, molten stone. Whether by volcanoes, faults or fissures and left to time and erosion, this is a trash-heap world of cooled ash and cinder. Across the stone fields, I gawk at the rock pavements and struggle across this moonscape rubble for most of the afternoon.

Given the chance to create a landscape with no holds barred, your imagination running wild, no creative mind could conjure a world this originally inventive, an inexhaustible beauty, an omnipresent loneliness.

Some of the pavements are crushed gray gravel, with larger black volcanic blobs of pitted boulders pressed into its surface, but polished bright and shining like shoes from the elements. The washes are just trenches of rounded smaller bowlers fit perfectly together, and great ironwood and palo verde spring from the stony beds. All this chaos, leaving quite an impression.

To my surprise, a great blue heron is discovered in a waterless wash—not a drop of water for a hundred miles.

The wind begins to die down, for which I am most thankful, as I am quite tired of chasing my hat with every wind gust. Having traversed these low foothills of the Bates Mountains, I make it to the Growler Wash. Kino Peak is the dominating topographic feature, and I know that I'm closing in on Bates Well and none too soon.

I am hurting, and pushing my body to its physical limits. My left foot is totally gone; not being able to apply any pressure on it, I walk with an exaggerated limp. The right lower leg, where it meets the foot, feels like a nail has been driven into the adjoining ligaments. My shoulders are a fist full of knotted muscles, my lower back bruised by the weight of carried water. Despite the torture I tolerate the inclination to lie down and die, having no choice but to press on.

The Growler Wash is a major river course; though waterless, there are times, though it's hard to believe, when water pours through this pass like the mighty Colorado. The high-water mark of debris, clings to some desert-brooms well outside of the wide stream bed. The torrents have carved and gouged out great pockets in the sandy beds, the size of trucks, that after the initial rush of water, are holding tanks, until the sand drinks it dry, leaving powder-dry, mud-cracked craters as I find them now.

Walking over the dune-soft sand is like walking up a down escalator, or swimming against the tide. I'm making progress but it's negligible. Jungles of thorny brush exist where the sand doesn't, and it is equally hard to negotiate, but with the struggle, I'm putting some miles behind me.

Distance in this desert world can be deceiving. Something that appears quite close, might be ten miles off, or things you could reach out and touch, could be a walk of two days. One can never be sure. I'm growing unsure once again.

Having walked now a good distance up the Growler Wash and judging my progress by Kino Peak, knowing the ranger station and Bates Well lie close to this landmark, and in this wash somewhere, I must be all but home. So dropping my pack, I climb up a rocky slope to an aerial view of my position. For the next few moments, my world came crashing in.

"Out of the abundance of the heart, the mouth speaks." I hope the Lord isn't listening, for more than a few imprecations have passed my lips this day. Out of sheer frustration and fatigue, faith falters.

As far as the eye can see up the wash, there are no signs of life. No road; it can't be far. No windmills; they should be right here. Have I come all the way up this pass, only to have missed what I've come for? Like everything else in the last few days, nothing has been where it should be, or thought it would be. Fortunately, I'm not lost, but I don't know where the hell I am. My exhaustion complete, my spirit broken. Profanity sootheth not the savage beast.

No option but to keep walking. A mystery as to where I find the strength. A few more miles . . . just a few more miles! After an appropriate distance, I climb another slope. And what to my wondering eyes should appear, an American flag! Praise God Almighty! I wonder, can I go the distance before dark? I do. Though not in short order, my doddering transports to the gates of the city, two trailers, three windmills, one American flag. Since the first mornings light, I have walked the day, long. I am very tired. Very tired.

As I enter, a frail old couple are huddled over a rusting oil drum and are bagging ashes. Setting down my backpack unnoticed, I walk over and say hello. They seem almost as surprised as I that others also live and breathe, equally excited and relieved to be able to talk to someone other than our own selves.

Explaining my situation, my hope of getting a ride from someone traveling this road back to Ajo, or any other place for that matter and of my adventure of the last four days, they invite me in for some coffee.

It's like old home week. They are warm and friendly and I the prodigal son. It is quickly decided that since tomorrow is their day off, and they'll be going to Ajo anyway, I should ride along. I have not the strength to argue and it's settled. Inside a small trailer, around a tiny table, the coffee is sweet and the conversation warm. The sun goes down as I listen to an endless string of great stories.

Roy and Fran Camper, a brother and sister team, are the caretakers here at Bates Well, permanent residents of what remains of the historic ranch. If left unattended, the ranch house and windmills and stock pens would be destroyed, so the government makes sure someone is always watching. Having worked in the Joshua Tree National Monument for a number of years in a similar capacity, they were transferred down to Organ Pipe and have been enjoying their retirement just hanging around. They're filled with the stories I love to hear.

Like the time a jaguar came in for a drink at the water trough. They are practically extinct, at least north of the border, but one stopped in for a sip and then quickly retreated into the great outback that surrounds this two-person outpost. What Roy called white Mexican fish wolves, up from the Gulf have done the same, as well as deer and big horn sheep. I am too tired to speak, but am suddenly alive with these tales.

"You must stay for dinner," says Fran as she slips some chicken pot pies into the oven. And Roy's stories unfold as a continual string of pearls. A retired Navy man has a lot to tell, covering a lot of conversational territory; music, wilderness, California, Arizona, guns, smugglers, poachers, illegal aliens, weather, mining, the Park Service, and on it goes. Dinner disappears but the stories don't and the evening rolls on.

No television there on the ranch, just the radio. Fran likes to listen to the "Radio Play House." It's time for the show. And Jimmy Stewart is starring in the "Shooter" and we're transported back to the 40's and totally entertained with the footsteps, door slams, and Jimmy's distinctive stammer. All this, adding to the quaintness of the evening. Later on it's a detective story, as we wonder who done it. Then it's more coffee and Roy rambles on till midnight. They tell me that they sleep late into the morning. I tell them I'll take a walk and see them whenever. "Pleasant dreams" as I step out of the trailer and into my sleeping bag.

I close my eyes and when I open them, it's morning. I am in no rush to get up; I am barely able. Around 10:00 A.M. I have some breakfast, as a coyote watches from across the drive. I manage to stand, hobble about for a short walk along the Growler Wash, and climb a mountainside.

From the heights, I look out across the Pass and beyond, out across the Growler Valley and the arena of my struggle. I've got the blues about not accomplishing what I've set out to do. A little embarrassed to tell friends of my failure. Try to console myself with the thought, that this defeat has been a learning experience. After all, it's easy to get lost, when you don't know where you're going.

Downing the slopes, exploring the ranch remains, a stock yard, a water tank, and bunk house. I am just too physically spent to do anything but sit down. Wander back to the trailer, sit by the water trough, and watch birds come in for a drink. Try to write a few notes; even this requires too much effort.

Around 3:00 P.M. Roy and Fran are beginning to stir. Late sleepers for sure! After their breakfast they invite me in for some coffee, and the stories begin again. One interesting note. In a small book in which they keep the daily temperature, wind and rain, I scan the records. Summer temperatures average 107, with hot days as high as 114. Less than three inches of rain for the year, yet many times, they have seen the Growler Wash run like a raging river. The water they use for coffee is pumped up by the windmill just thirty-five feet below the surface.

At 4:00 P.M. we jump into a pickup and head up the rough-and-tumble road twenty miles to Ajo. Stopping at the pharmacy to get some medicine for Fran's back and after picking up some groceries, they insist on dinner. Fran says, "It's a long ride back to Tucson."

After a relaxing dinner and more of Ray's stories, they won't even let me pick up the check. Hate to see this come to an end. They've become my surrogate parents. I know they were pleased to have a visitor come to call, in their remote world. Back into the pickup for the short ride down to "Why" and my waiting truck.

It's many good-byes, a hug from Fran and a Merry Christmas wish. The adventure draws to a close.

In four days of walking, I've covered sixty miles. Learned some lessons about the lay of the land and the weight of water. Apart from the serious pain in my left foot, that will take two weeks to get back to normal, its been a good experience.

In the years to come, I will make several more cross-country trips back into the Growler Valley and become better acquainted with this empty desert. In retrospect, I can't believe I made the mistakes I did on this walk.

It is laughable to think you can walk very far, carrying six gallons of water. I knew that going in. But not being familiar enough with the lay of the land at the time, or the proprietor of an appropriate vehicle that might transport me to a halfway point, where I could cache water, which is the only way this walk can be accomplished, I hoped that my physical prowess would be enough. It is not enough. I am not Superman.

The other blunder was in being far less concerned about the first two valleys I had to cross than about the formidable wasteland of the Pinacate, the last half of the big journey. Misinterpreting the Agua Dulce Mountains with the Sierras southeast of Lukeville on the Mexican side, led me to far to the west of my intended destination and many unnecessary miles eastward to discover I wasn't where I thought I was.

Often I have wondered how I would have fared carrying just four gallons. Winter temperatures are mild and water requirements not as great. Even with my directional mistakes, the Pinacate lay just a hair beyond my view. Once that mountain was sighted, I would have known exactly where I was. Would I have had the strength at that point to continue? This is sheer speculation and water over the dam. I live with my mistakes.

One thing was for certain; after four days and sixty miles, I was incapable of going any farther. Even had I put these miles in the right direction, I would still have forty plus miles to go and therein lies the rub.

The Growler Wash has long been a corridor through which ancient man journeyed. A few miles east of Bates Well, there are very clear petroglyphs carved on the black volcanic boulders above the arroyo. A kind of sign-post, at a migratory crossroads.

As for the men who fashioned them, who lived and walked across these deserts and down to the sea, modern man, with all his convenience and technology, can't begin to comprehend their world. It could not have been a life of abundance. They were forced to be minimalists; this spare landscape would have seen to that. But they knew something that we don't. How to live within the perimeters of what the land could provide. The fact that they did it successfully for millennia is a testament to the endurance of the human spirit.

The western deserts of Arizona and northwestern Sonora Mexico are wonderfully unique, emaciated and austere, with a charm all their own. Because they're so open and spacious; it's fun and quite easy, when it's not hot, when you're not carrying much water, to walk a great distance over this terrain in a day. So I keep coming back and I keep walking.

In conclusion: those deserts are very serious business. Only a fool travels there in the summer. Treat them with the respect they are due. They are places, scary big and empty. Many have lost their lives there. Proceed with caution.

Going . . . Going . . . Gone

Before this city came sprawling
Before this desert was filled
With streets and homes
Before the rivers stopped running
Before the traffic stood still
Before the Spanish
In search of their cities of gold
Before the Anglo came stealing
Before the snow-bird took wing
In search of a home
Before the natives lost theirs
God made this beautiful place.

But it's going . . . going . . . gone.

Now I know that the Lord
Has made the world a field
Raising folks up to Heaven
Through the Son he revealed
But I can't help but worry
As we plunder and sack
That this place won't be ruined
By the time he gets back.

'Cause it's going . . . going.

Gone the simple red man dreaming
Come the population teeming
Gone the open space and air
Complete with modern man's despair
Gone the hope we'll one day see
A land more glorious wild and free.

'Cause its going . . . going . . . gone.

Before this city came sprawling
Before this desert was filled
With streets and homes
Before the rivers stopped running
Before the traffic stood still
Before the Spanish
In search of their cities of gold
Before the Anglo came stealing
Before the snow-bird took wing
In search of a home
Before the natives lost theirs
God blessed this land and this place.

But it's going . . . going . . . gone.
1986

Buehman Creek, Santa Catalina Mountains.

Buehman Creek

Buehman Creek is the only living stream on the eastern face of the Santa Catalina Mountains; that in and of itself, makes it an extraordinary phenomenon, the only flowing water on a huge tract of empty desert filled with creosote and saguaros. What is also unbelievable, on the southern and northwestern faces of the Catalinas, there are nearly a million people living. I have spent many years walking and taking photographs in this canyon, and I share them with you here.

I'll let the images do the talking. Keep coming back and shooting my favorite locations again and again. What is a constant source of amazement to me, in a place you might think would remain reasonably static, the exact opposite is true. It is a land that is in a constant state of flux and metamorphosis. Not in a subtle way but dramatically, not every now and then, but on a near daily basis.

A major flood will move through the canyon, erasing stream-side thickets of cottonwood and willow, rearranging the beaches and reefs of river rock. Seedlings will quickly establish themselves. In a handful of years, those seedlings are eighteen feet high. Full-fledged trees. A woodland, near impenetrable. A big storm will stall over the Catalinas and a ten-foot wall of water will sweep through the canyon, vaporizing those forests, leaving a few, aesthetically well-chosen trees, and the process begins anew. Places where the stream was a babbling brook flowing over cobblestones, can quickly be replaced by an Olympic-sized pool of waist-deep water.

What at first appears to be complete destruction is actually a blessing, just as fire is both destructive and beneficial to a forest. Floods do the same for desert streams, not only enhancing the canyon visually, but creating better fish habitat, improving the woodlands themselves and fashioning a healthier environment for every living thing that ties itself to this and other similar, magically watered canyons.

96

The witchery of color and light; igniting the rock promontories, the wild and opposing combinations of desert plant and stream-side woodland. The seductive incantation of these talking tinseled waters, brings a potpourri of fish, bird, animal and plant, that cannot exist without this wellspring. For beyond this wet sanctuary is nothing but a desert.

The spiritual implications for me are undeniable: a desert without an oasis is like a man without the Lord.

These remaining desert streams are spellbindingly beautiful and worth far more than money. Seeing is believing.

Please Pardon Me Please

There's a field out there I'm gonna to walk it
A feelin' easy blowin' on the breeze
There's a field out there I'm gonna to walk it
Pardon me please.

There's a chance out there I've got to take it
For it's this moment that each one of us must seize
There's a chance out there I'm gonna take it
Please pardon me please.

There's a longin' that a sailor knows
That sets those ships to sea
A snow goose sailin' when the seasons change. . . .
It's got to go . . . it's got to be
I've got that hobo personality. . . .
I'm an explorer extraordinaire
Yes, I'm that man . . . yes, I'm that free
Please pardon me please.

There are mountains that climb
Into the heavens
A benediction this sojourner can't ignore
If the wilderness should call. . . .
I'm bound to listen
'Cause I'm wantin' more . . . more . . . more
There's a river somewhere cuttin' canyons
And with a boat I'm gonna take her to the sea
Rivers roll and I'm bound to roam
It's bye-bye . . . you're wavin' to me.

Pardon me . . . this traffic is too frustratin'
Pardon me . . . this wanderer's heart's-a-palpitatin'
Pardon me . . . it's my leave I must be takin'. . . .
Pardon me.

There's a longin' that a sailor knows
That sets those ships to sea
A snow goose sailin' when the seasons change. . . .
It's got to go . . . it's got to be
I've got that hobo personality. . . .
I'm an explorer extraordinaire
Yes, I'm that man . . . yes, I'm that free
Please pardon me please.

There are mountains out there. . . .
There's a river somewhere
There's a field out there I'm gonna to walk it
Pardon me please . . . please pardon me please.
1988

White Canyon Wilderness, north of the Gila River.

Bobcats in Bonita

The Gila river tumbles out of New Mexico and cuts its way through Arizona's eastern mountains, before spilling across the broad Gila Valley, to water the cotton fields and the farming community of Safford. A dirt road skirts the waterway, as it knifes through the Gila Box, a 29,000-acre, National Riparian Conservation Area.

A small sign points the way to Bonita Creek. For miles I climb up the arcing hills that have muscled in on the river. The wrinkled landscape undulates; mountains rounded hills, canyonous folds between the ridges. Creosote springs from the stony ground and the sparse grass over the collective acres, stain the hillsides in olives and golds.

At the crest of the wave, I park the truck by a corral and peer off the brink. The flesh of the desert has been sliced wide open, with the cutting blade still in the open wound, down the plunging slopes to the barranca floor and the tranquil stream Bonita.

A four-wheel-drive road and the creek braid their way up the canyon. With my late arrival (This is a day walk, I've already driven 130 miles from Tucson), I have to march in as far as I can and be back before dark. The day bejeweled and the walking easy.

Stratus clouds gauze a blue sky and the rock walls part like the biblical waters of the Red Sea. Mature cottonwoods mark time on wide gravel beaches and the summer cloak of skeletal sycamores crunch underfoot. The sun streaming through occasional canopies of walnut and the familiar musk of willow hangs in the air. Fish at my feet when I wade the crystal stream.

The "Anasazi" lived here centuries ago, the "Apaches" after them, the latter using Bonita as an escape route from San Carlos, when they would jump the reservation for their illegal Mexican forays. Today Bonita is famed for its large raptor populations. I've come to watch the feathered predators fly the rim-rock.

After some miles the red rock walls close in, restricting visibility. A layer of long-johns takes the chill off the shadowed hallway,

101

the afternoon sun gliding canyon rims, where creosote arms bob in the breeze and red-tail hawks patrol.

Life is a puzzle. Often I feel I'm the one piece that doesn't fit. Today I find a niche, treading through the canyon at a fast clip, in the usual euphoric state this walking brings.

A resolute march of two and a half hours brings me to a large park where two large drainages enter the creek, on either side, the valley planted with a mesquite bosque and well-spaced sycamore and cottonwood. The creek is a vein of silver shining in the sun, a scarab of jade this planted garden, set in the cleft of the rounded rise of treeless hills.

I would keep going, but time does not allow. Halfway back through the corridor, a rock falls from a canyon wall. To my surprise, two large bobcats are coming down to the stream.

One stands on a ledge broadside, with a stance like a show-dog. I'm convinced they see me, but they keep climbing down. I step into a screen of desert-brooms, in the hopes of seeing the cats cross the creek. Disappearing for a moment, I hear them crunching through the leaf litter and the green wall of growth stream-side. A second later they walk out of the brush at my feet! Never looking up or giving any indication that they know I'm there.

I follow them down the road for a quarter mile. With each bend they're a little farther afield, with another turn they're gone. Carefree and confident, princely and powerful; in their weight class, they're the kings of the jungle. I'm glad I'm not a rabbit in the neighborhood.

The day draws to a close. I huff and puff with the steep climb out of the canyon, to catch the sun's last rays beaming over the profile of the Gila Mountains. On the shoulders of the canyon's eastern walls, Turtle Mountain stands naked in the last light's blush.

Down the river rock slopes to the Gila, a green gray ribbon twisting through the deepening lavender hills. I leave the water running and bobcats to hunt under a sliver of moon.

I'm Just a Cowboy

The night so pleasant when the moon shines bright
You'll see forever through a desert night
Halfway to Mexico . . . the Santa Ritas insight
And I got lucky when I found a home
With all these open places here to roam
I climb the mountains high. . . .
I search the deserts below.

I'm just a cowboy . . . I've got a song to sing
I feel the joy life brings as I ride across the plain
The sun and the rain. . . .
Like a color-slide changin' . . .
Bringin' motion to the land
Like the changes the years bring. . . .
The feelin's that seem to spring
From where this cowboy takes his stand.

I see the mountains standin' white in the winter. . . .
Shinin' wet when it rains
I see the Lord's work plainly. . . .
On a land stretchin' endlessly
And lately . . . I've got to walk somewhere. . . .
I've got to go.

The days so pleasant and the summers long
A cowboy dreams of girls . . . a horse . . . a song
And a love he might find to share. . . .
Singin' songs in the sun
If he's lucky, well, he'll find her there. . . .
Cool Senorita with the long dark hair
It's love deep that he'll find himself. . . .
Under cottonwood trees.

She's just a cowgirl . . . she's just a fool like me
She'd drive to Hart Prairie. . . .
Just to say that she'd been there
She'd wait if she had too. . . .
For me on some barstool. . . .
I'm singin' longer than I planned
She brings a joy as the years go. . . .
Good lovin' that seems to flow
From where these cow-kids take their stand.

I hope she sees me walkin'
Lonesome some canyon. . . .
Singin' songs in her dreams
'Cause I hear a song quite plainly. . . .
An endless melody. . . .
And lately I've got to play somewhere.

I'm just a cowboy . . . I've got a song to sing
I feel the joy life brings . . . as I ride across the plain
The sun and the rain. . . .
Like a color-slide changin'. . . .
Bringin' motion to the land
Like the changes the years bring. . . .
The feelin's that seem to spring
From where this cowboy takes his stand.

The nights so pleasant when the moon shines bright.
1979

The Plains of Sonoita, Cienaga Creek Preserve.

Cienaga Creek

Cienaga Creek starts its flow at the Canelo Hills in southern Arizona and runs north across the plains of Sonoita to the Rincons, its source some thirty miles from old Mexico. Bordered on the east by the Whetstone Mountains and on the west by the Santa Ritas, lies a stunning sweep of seemingly endless prairie, covering four hundred square miles of Montana-like grassland, framed on all sides by grand blue mountains whose forested slopes ooze onto the plain like syrup in the sun, to form the shore of an ocean of grass, that writhes and rolls where the wind wills. And it calls the cowboy, like a sailor, to ply his trade on the open waters.

Silver shafts of sunlight play on the shining sea of grass. Sculpted cumulus troop across the fathomless dome of blue, as the cloud shadows change the countenance of the mountains' proud profiles and with it the oscillating moods of the waist-deep waters.

Along the bottom of this gigantic valley runs a small ribbon of water, its shores garlanded with cottonwood, walnut, and willow, which decorates as it descends the valley perfect and peaceful. This place is an Arizona scenic jewel, a rancher's nirvana, a cowboy's waking dream. Everyone's vision of what the West should be and ought to be. Within this valley and its bordering mountains, the history of the American West unfolded.

Twenty miles to the east, Coronado led a thousand men down the San Pedro River Valley in 1540, in search of golden cities, discovering nothing but disappointment. The very ground on which they walked housed millions in silver and three hundred years later would produce the boom towns of Tombstone and Harshaw. Money brought gunfighters, gamblers, the honest and the lawless.

To the east Father Kino established his missions for God and King, along the Santa Cruz River, and opened up the way for the trapper, miner, the rancher and the dreamer. They sought to explore and exploit whatever they could find for the taking.

The California 49ers drank from Cienaga's waters as they

headed west for their imagined bonanza. The Butterfield Stage and the railroad crossed and trestled its course. The infamous Apache Wars were all fought within and round its perimeters. A thousand stories told and untold, real and imagined, grew to legend in proportion to the size of the landscape and live in the hearts of every American to this day.

Little has changed since the days of the Spanish explorers. Since the glory days of the eighteen hundreds, when a man with guts and a gun could test himself against the wilderness, and with a little luck, come out not only with his life, but with money and a name.

Today the speculative prospector wears a coat and tie and mines money from wealthy Easterners, who move to the burgeoning Sunbelt cities like Tucson, in search of the good life. With Tucson bursting its borders just forty miles to the northwest, any real estate developer worth his salt sees Cienaga's fair valleys as something to be exploited, as did former generations, but this time not with mining claims or cows, but with condos, shopping malls, and golf courses.

As fate would have it or call it Divine Providence, the government has purchased the Empire Cienaga Creek Ranch holdings of some fifty thousand acres through the heart of the valley. In this way its ground water, which measures millions upon millions of acre-feet, might be saved for Tucson's future needs, that the endangered species of Gila Minnow, that school in Cienaga's waters might be protected. To keep away the ruthless realtors, who would sell their souls for a piece of the action, that this pristine portion of paradise, might remain as it has since time began.

It is for certain that I am not a sailor and a cowboy only in spirit. I have set a course to walk the thirty-five-mile river. To see first hand the Bureau of Land Managements purchase of Cienaga Creek. To test myself against the landscape's colored contours and see what bounty the river possesses. To answer the call of this strange and persistent longing. To come walk the wild places.

Recruiting the services of my next-door neighbors for the ride east from Tucson, the interstate flung us like a sling shot projectile, away from the confusion and chaos of the metropolitan morass. Away from the discontented city dwellers, cursing their lot and the

107

evening traffic, to leave us free and flying across the creosote flats. Soon the city, just as unpleasant memory.

I point with excitement to the mountains that ring the horizon, now bold blue blocks of color. The strange glow of the pastel desert floor, contrasting the ceramic blue sky. The odd shapes of the luminous, pearl-colored clouds. It is a typical evening in this Southwest wonderland. They do not notice the beauty. I'm embarrassed I brought it up. We talk of other things. The car rolls on approaching ground zero.

We arrive at the point where cienaga empties its waters into the Pantano Wash and to deserts farther below. There the river ends its northerly flow, as the interstate intersects its course and continues eastward. The car pulls over, we say good-bye; they cruise back to Tucson. I am up a creek.

It's already late as the sun hastens to end the day before I can put in too many miles. I stumble over the cobblestones and dry sandbars. Soon the clouds are kindled to molten metal and a three-quarter moon helps extend twilight, letting me push on a bit farther. Just beyond a working ranch, so that I won't be seen, set up the tent and do dinner.

Once a few years ago, on another walk in the Whetstone Mountains, not far from my present location, I came across a bunch of working cowboys complete with tents, fires, branding irons, and very angry eyes. I was told to get out! Convinced they were going to start shooting. I want to avoid such confrontations.

I fall asleep under moonbeams, with the doggies mooing and eighteen-wheelers whizzing down the interstate some miles off.

I open my eyes at dawn. After a breakfast of oatmeal and tea; I break camp. I start up the dry river leaving the ranch and the cows behind.

There the river walls run just a few feet high. Low desert hills flank its sides, decorated with ocotillo, creosote, mesquite, and a good amount of grass. We've had a good monsoon this year, and the desert blushes green.

The wash swings and sways, first this way and that. I try to walk as straight a line as possible, climbing up on the reefs and bars, forcing my way through the brush, then into the channel as it swings back around, wondering how far I'll go before water starts flowing.

I rejoice in the cool morning air, the baby blue cloudless sky, the new day's yellow light, as it plays on the ocotillo arms that silently watch from the bluffs above my head. Small birds work the undergrowth; apart from their singing and the crunch of gravel under my feet, there are no other sounds. Miles unfold.

Quite unexpectedly a small puddle with a few minnows. Not more than twenty yards upstream, the river began flowing, as though someone had turned on a spigot. At the water's edge where it disappeared into the sand, minnows swam and played. From that point on, the river, which prior to this was no river at all, was suddenly a waterway filled with promise. I marvel at the fish, the surprising amount of water tumbling over the rocks on the wide stream bed, noting the soothing voice of the waters as they made their descent. Thought about the spiritual implications of water flowing across a dry land.

I will make a way in the wilderness and rivers in the desert.
Isaiah 43:19

I estimate my position at perhaps twelve miles from the interstate. It's 10:00 A.M., already tired. Moving another half mile, crashing into the stream bed, breaking into the munchies, beef sticks, candy and carrots, punctuated by great gulps of water. I take a few minutes rest, click a few photographs, and inventory my surroundings.

Growth along the flood plain is thickening. Jungles of mesquite line the stream banks, small walnut trees have appeared, and willow bend their boughs and shade the flowing waters that beckon farther exploration. I strap on the backpack and stumble on.

Going nowhere fast. The river is forcing its way through low elongated parallel hills, forming "S" shapes and right angles. With each turn and bend, the river has a different personality. In one place the water is 30 feet wide and 2 inches deep, or it's a trench 3 feet wide and 2 feet deep. Water is tumbling over rock shelves, gushing over gravel beds, or growing pockets of quicksand that impede my increasingly labored steps.

Red-tail hawks patrolling the sky. Squadrons of hummingbirds working the nearby flowerbeds. Yellow-breasted finches flashing from the tree tops. Conventions of butterflies convening on the sand banks, some mating on the wing, in every color of the rainbow. Gigantic prehistoric-size dragonflies running reconnaissance missions along the water's edge. Miles unfold.

An intense bright sun is burning the back of my neck, like an electric iron, placed on permanent press, as I drag a ball and chain. I believe it to be a scientific principle; pack weight increases in direct proportion to the number of miles incurred. Shoulder straps are cutting like surgical blades through ham hocks.

A great gray heron spreads in the silent wings and moves upstream, preferring to dine alone. I seek the shade of a walnut tree, rest and lunch.

The morning desert landscape falls away. After scaling a twenty-foot waterfall, I step onto a rolling savanna, an emerald prairie. Grandiose cottonwood dot the flatland pastures. Oak and mesquite fill the seams on the rolling hills beyond. The 7,400-foot Whetsone Mountains form a bold backdrop, as the sky brews storm and thunderhead.

This is the last of the sweeping landscape I will see until the late afternoon hours. The runnel has bored its way through prairie sediments and carved a canyon fifteen feet deep, from which there is no escape for myself, or the stream. Within its confines, explore an inter-world of beauty. I take guesses at whose tracks are pressed into the sand, delicate little hands and feet, javelina, coyotes and ringtail cats.

Time passing. Through the bends and the nooks, Cienaga Creek drags and drifts, trickling lazily along.

I spy a great horned owl. His big eyes watch from a rotating head as I push my way through a patch of black-eyed Susans below his perch. Then, with a boom of thunder, the sky opens up. I welcome the rain and the rest, seeking shelter in a thicket of cottonwood.

For hours I have been marching. Approaching physical exhaustion, I sadistically enjoy the pain. I'm dirty, muddy, and soaked to the skin—and strangely content. Miles from nowhere and a kid in a candy shop. Beyond this valley rages an ugly city stuffed with people, with its concrete, cars, and "Circle K" convenience stores. I can scarcely believe that fact is true. Civilization is marching on without me. Delighted with the prospect.

The storm passes, sun shafts beam down on the water course.

Diamond raindrops sparkling, set the trees, the rocks, and the grasses to glistening like a million mirrors. I set out again through a steaming wet jungle. A few more turns and another mile, suddenly free of the river's prison walls.

Before me is the most idyllic ranch scene the mind could conjure. Bountiful fenced pastures, gigantic cottonwoods, blue blobs, against gorgeous green hills, that rise up one upon another, like ocean swells, held in check by the forested peaks of the Santa Ritas and the Whetstones miles distant. With the ranch houses, the barns and windmills, it's a pastoral tapestry that gladdens the eye, and a vision of the Promised Land.

A dirt road parallels the river, the ranch, and beyond. I take advantage of the uncluttered path to find the ranch abandoned. This may be the Empire Cienaga Creek Ranch, but without a map, I cannot tell. Would anyone leave a place this beautiful? Perhaps they have been called, as unto Heaven.

The road turns west, I know not where. I crash through the willow thickets and back into the water. The river is suddenly not a river at all. Stalled in a depression among the hills, I'm in the Florida Everglades. With Herculean effort, I struggle through mud and muck to my knees. Trapped, like a mastodon, in the La Brea Tar Pits. Clouds of mosquitoes move in for the kill. Scrambling to the shore, there is nothing but a wilderness of grass seven feet tall and no escape. Headlines flash before me: "Unsuccessful songwriter, found dead, in bizarre wilderness mishap."

After thirty minutes, or an hour, or several lifetimes, I break the chains of the swamp, climbing up on some hills away from the mud and mosquitoes. There is a thunderstorm pouring over the Whetstone Mountains with the power of a nuclear blast. In a blowing gale. I set up the tent and the deluge begins.

I am totally spent and lie like a corpse and listen to the rain.

Take a walk after dinner upon my ridge above the river. There is a glory of color that rests upon this land, a beauty that passeth understanding, that touches the spirit to wonder and worship. Dark brooding clouds are throwing lightning bolts at the Whetstone Mountains, and blue curtains of rain are falling on its slopes, bringing out the colors in the rolling savanna so green that it is permanently dyed into my memory. Not a landscape more perfect, this side of Heaven.

And there was evening and there was morning, a second day.

The morning's clear light finds the birds singing their rejoicing anthems to a new day. Across the Elysian fields and rhythmical flow of hills, wreaths of clouds hide the conifer forests of the Santa Ritas. Below me a silver string of water, calling as an invocation. I break camp, as the adventure continues.

Yesterday's swamp struggle is a bad dream. The river opens up again and flows effortlessly across the grassland. With unbridled enthusiasm, I splash through the morning under a spell of inspiration. There is great beauty here. I am in love. There are no words.

Another gray heron leaps from the willow canopy and gracefully doubles back over the trees. Hawks are working the skies above the range, killdeer the water's edge. Across the fertile valley, horizons of mountain and mist. Think of the bear that call it home, of lions that leave those peaks ragged and torn, to seek a kill on these plains below.

The price of admittance to this show is a physical test. Cienaga regains its high walls and a slow run, a marshy course filled with bulrushes and water lily-like plants. I take turns swimming through the soup, or forcing my way along the top, where grass stands over my head. I startle a drove of deer along the carved cliff walls and they bound on springboards into the thickets. One of Arizona's largest white-tailed deer herds call this valley home. If you can see them, you're a taller man than I.

The river's flow ends just as it began. Above a small puddle teeming with minnows, there is nothing but a gravel bed. The spigot is turned off, the flow stops at the tap, and the water is no more.

Morning miles have taken their toll. Out of gas. I lounge on the sands, tank up on sunflower seeds and Snickers bars, relishing the shade of a cottonwood and mourning the death of the river.

I give the city not a thought. I drift into dreams, pondering the big questions, the ones past finding out, the wonder of it all. My ignorance is bliss.

Cienaga Creek is a dry wash now, a driveway of smooth gravel banked by lush green grass. Roadrunners dart to and fro, and quail like shotgun blasts, explode from the green borders. The cottonwood and mesquite that peppered the savanna along the way, disappear completely with the miles. A Nebraskan prairie rolls on as far as the eye can see.

Growing weary of the wash's confines and seeing the direction I should go, I set a course across the mantle of grass. There is great freedom in open spaces like these. Fly and float, drift effortless across the grass gardens like the cumulus clouds above me. The proportion and sweep of the landscape is overwhelming, under a marvelous light, and the rolling ridges change their moods with the sky. The afternoon and the miles go by; a great distance is covered.

Crossing an Arizona Serengeti, Mount Wrightson, the 9,400-foot summit of the Santa Ritas, a Kilimanjaro. I search the plains for elephants and wildebeest, but the only thing that's moving are some cattle on distant hills, the grass at my feet, clouds whizzing overhead. There's a healthy herd of pronghorn antelope that graze this grass, but they are sailing some other quadrant of this ocean.

In the late afternoon, I set up camp about a mile and a half from Route #82, a road running west from the small city of Sierra Vista beyond this valley, to the tiny community of Sonoita, set upon the hill from which Cienaga starts its flow. My journey soon over.

Dinner is enjoyed in the bright light of a sunshower, the eastern sky a black curtain as double-arc semicircle rainbows frame the grassland buttes, in an Ansel Adams vision of Wyoming.

After my meal, walk the rolling swells and flowering glades transfixed by the power and pageantry of a thunderstorm as it terrorizes high mountain slopes, clothed in blue cumulus and lightning. Searchlights like sunbeams, poured through the cloud holes, solid as rays of steel. In places such as this, I'm convinced there are no disbelievers.

In the blue evening shadows of twilight, hear the thunder of hoofs. Up over a rise not twenty feet away at first, fly fifteen pronghorn, and the feeling is rapturous. There is an animal that looks like it stepped off the African plain, but these mercurial creatures are an American original. Antelope have roamed this valley since time began, designed to wander far and free and at great speed, or stand quietly for uninvited guests. A primeval experience, honored and humbled to be in their presence.

A full moon lights the prairie dancing.

And there was evening and there was morning, a third day.

113

In the morning, I walk the final few miles across the prairie, observing the last twists and turns of dry Cienaga as it makes its way to its source, a small basin in the graceful grassy hills. In the small town of Sonoita, I stick out my thumb and catch a ride back to civilization. The odyssey draws to a close.

I know of no one who has walked the length of this river. It is not on the itinerary of things people aspire to do. I will cherish the accomplishment.

Tucson is as I left it. Cars crowd the ugly streets. Drivers jockey for pointless position at the traffic lights. Myriads mill in the malls. The city like a cancer grows. The good life goes on.

I can't help but think . . . if the earth is our mother . . . we have broken the fifth commandment.

I have drunk deep from Cienaga's waters and the beauty of the valley, and in walking through it, I have participated with and become one with the enchanted landscape. It is locked into all my senses. Hopelessly infatuated with the glory of it all, this love is a thing experienced, not rationally explained.

The Bureau of Land Management's purchase of the Empire Cienaga Creek Ranch is an act of which I wholeheartedly approve. I know a good buy when I see one. It's comforting to know that in a world where twentieth century man consumes wild places like he does fast food, this river valley will be protected. Life will continue, as it has since the day the Lord set this sphere to spinning, along a watercourse called Cienaga.

Mountain Songs

I never understood the city. . . .
Why anyone would choose to stay.

Soon the mountains will be rising
From a plain grand and sweeping
Standing high where the snow's rarely gone
Far above trees there standing. . . .
Lies the tundra cold but handing over streams
Now they're starting to flow. . . .
Cutting deep the tortured canyon course
A siren song that calls
And forces me to climb and see
It's of color space and time astounding. . . .
Pastures, forests skies abounding
You know I believe in mountain songs. . . .
You're never down for long with a mountain song
Mountain songs. . . .
Give up those city throngs for a mountain song.

Now there's something in the wilderness. . . .
For me there's no describing
On the trail those urban blues are gone
It's the wonder in the canyons glowing. . . .
Freedom in the storm that's growing
Joy in those stars at the end of a day
I know a peace, like by those streams I'm walking. . . .
The Lord I hear when nature's talking
His hand in all I see. . . .
My heart's a song in praise to all its glory
And until the day the Lord should call me. . . .
You know where I'll be
Singing mountain songs. . . .
You can't be down for long with a mountain song
Mountain songs. . . .
Give up those city throngs for a mountain song

I never understood the city. . . .
Why anyone would choose to stay.
1987

Sotols, Galiuro Mountains.

Pipestem Canyon

The Mercer Ranch rests in a small valley behind Sombero Butte and the western walls of the Galiuro Mountains. A mining road lances up the slopes as I inch along beneath the wincing weight of a backpack. Make a vow, I will never carry water again.

In less than two miles, there are blisters on my heels the size of half-dollars. I've walked a thousand miles of wild Arizona, no problem. Today there's a new rub. The damage done, mole-skins provide an ineffective veneer against increased pain and suffering.

I leave the road, maneuvering up a sharp rock face crowded with brush and stunted oak, then up open slopes to the mountain's crown. A twenty-two hundred foot climb and a pleasant walk, but with a backpack, it's the hardest thing I've ever done.

From the summit stones, the 10,700-foot Pinaleno Mountains, beyond this range, are a distant blue wall with a mantel of white. The ground at my feet drops like a banner into Four Mile Creek; a ribbon of green oaks works down the drainage. The foreground a crumpled quilt of stony grass slopes, tumbling to Aravaipa. Oaks retreat into shaded dells, where even at 6,000 feet the sun sternly defines their borders. To the west the San Pedro River, a huge empty valley, minus the mining community of San Manuel, and the Santa Catalina Mountains.

I ride the arcing back of the mountain, drop over the other side, and meet the headwaters of Pipestem Canyon.

I walk an ancient landscape. Yesterday in Tucson they found the bones of a dead man three thousand years old, in the side of a riverbank. Seven thousand years before his death, Stone Age Clovis men were hunting mastodons in the valley below.

Arizona was cool and wet back then. In the intervening centuries, it grew hot and dry, the sun replacing trees with cactus, forests retreating to mountaintops, climbing into elevated canyons where a desert sun would not fall. Noting where trees grow here, is always an interesting study.

118

The canyon is a golden trough of grass hills without a tree, but in the seam is a generous oak forest, where trees stand thirty feet tall. In the distance a small pocket of pine is standing in the shadowed cleft of Rhodes Peak, a harbinger of wonderful discoveries to come.

I work down the steep drainage under a green canopy, braking onto a terrace above the trees and the stream, startling deer that disappear as quickly as they are seen.

Mad at myself for carrying this much water, with this much present. The last two days of rain have filled the rivulets with a gush. The burden I carry requires all I have. The hillsides are platinum-blond roofs; the trees in the drainages grow in the gutters. Silvered waters are tumbling down these roofs and the gutters are rattling.

I drop into a tributary rill, deposit my pack under a huge cedar, and nearly float into the air, freed from the weight. I leave my cross where it is and explore the neighborhood.

I hobble down the canyon, crippled by the blisters, looking for a possible campsite. But the ravine drops too steeply and is crammed with oak and cedar, farther down the Chihuahua pine, afternoon sun streaming through jungle branches, water tumbling over rocks with a roar.

I wander up the Crest Trail, climb two hundred feet to a bald plateau, perfect staging for my explorations. From here I can look up the canyon from whence I came. Down the huge canyon I hope to go and the path that leads to Rhodes is at my door.

I set up camp, gather wood, and climb a ridge, to watch the sun go down. With the last light, I look across the broken ledges of the Galiuros. This much wilderness makes me realize how much I'm committed and how alone I really am.

Beyond the fire's glow, there is nothing but darkness and the distant flicker of stars, later a moon.

With the morning I'm a centenarian. The day's course is along the Crest Trail. Rhodes Peak is a cap of rock and the high point on this ridge. An acre of pines linger in its shadowed northern exposures. Beyond this 7,100-foot mountaintop, where the sun presses hard, stunted oak and pinion pine, with tight tangles of manzanita, tumbling precipitously into deep-seamed canyons where wonderfully, and at five-thousand feet, there are stands of Douglas fir.

119

These mountains are a hinterland, as truly defined. No roads, no people, and rarely visited. The official wilderness is some 76,000 acres, but this is attached to an uninhabited chunk of real estate of almost a 1,000 square miles. The Sierra Club describes this landscape as primeval in character as any in the United States. When you wander in, you wander alone.

The land is so infrequently traveled that trails are almost non-existent. You walk along, sensing a path of faintest of impressions. I follow along for miles, as far as I perceive it going. Turn around where the stunted forest topples off the western escarpment.

I take my time on the way back, watching over the stern landscapes blue corrugations.

Completely spent from the rigors of the last two days, in the amphitheater I find myself camped, stretched out beside the tent, beneath the roofing arms of a juniper. In sunlight so intense, Heaven's light could not be brighter. It's windy and the grassy slopes breathe with the warm air. Melting as butter in a heated pan, I wonder whether it's a loss of strength or will, but it matters not, lying down is all I can muster.

After a rest, I limp about. I gather more wood. The blisters have ruined me. Up the golden hillsides to watch the sunset. Down the hill through the twilight for dinner, a fire, the moon.

I'm just a shadow with the morning. The best of the walk lays ahead. Pipestem drops steadily four to five miles down to Rattlesnake Canyon, through a forest of mixed conifer, wonderful to behold. The Galiuros are filled with anomalies of vegetation at strange elevations. Old growth stands of ponderosa line the canyon floor. I can't think of another timberland of this caliber and this low, anywhere else in southern Arizona. Small parks of isolated trees, hiding in the clefts of secluded ridges.

To walk these woodlands is to walk in the spirit, to marvel at creation and the aura of peace that forests exude. Big blobs of bear scat as I press through the understory. Oaks, cedars, yucca, maples, ponderosa, Douglas fir, agave and sycamore, wonderful collections these intricate gardens.

The miles unfold in a serpentine fashion and Pipestem spills into Rattlesnake. Lunch at the confluence, gaining some strength and proceeding up the main drag.

Water flows free over a wide stream bed, the canyon planted

like a garden, wide-open shelves beside the river. Wonderful esthetic tree groupings. A landscape artist could find his muse here and if he could capture its forlorn and haunt, he would be a master craftsman.

I'm in the heart of a vast chunk of wilderness, in the midst of topography so difficult, a virtual fortress against the outside world. Few scale its walls to plunder these visual treasures. It is place separated by more than just its cumbersome configuration and the physical distance one can measure to civilization. A less definable line is the mystery that enshrouds landscapes like these. We need places like this. It reminds us that the world is a place that we do and don't know anything about.

In the thickets deer appear; they graze, they love, and the pedigrees continue. Through the hot summers, bear forage and their cubs learn the ropes; in winter they can't stay awake. A lion leaps from the shadows, a deer is missing from the drove. A thousand years go by. No one knows and no one sees.

Beyond these mountains, deserts expand under the weight of huge cities. People drive their cars, live out their lives in comfortable houses, in ever-expanding convenience and technology. Neither citizen of either world knows of the other, or scarcely comprehends. I don't comprehend, though man there has been distracted and this primitive world remains. It's nice to know there's something this big, still untouched that one can wander into.

A half-mile up Rattlesnake, the water stops flowing. A driveway of smooth sand runs for miles up to Powers Garden and beyond. Bonnie and bone dry. This canyon is big, a watershed of perhaps 150 square miles, but try to find some water. To sojourn there, you'll have to walk. It's the only way, accomplished with sweat and hard work. Apart from the intimidating size of this back country and the unaccommodating topography, water is as hard to find as gold and worth considerably more. Come summer when it's over a hundred degrees, a man coming unprepared can find himself in big trouble.

I've had a few close calls in these mountains, when it's very hot and dry and completely devoid of any water. These life-threatening distances can be longer than one can possibly imagine.

A golden eagle lifts off a deer carcass thirty paces to my left and flies at chest level through the trees toward me, but slightly ahead.

121

With a determined step, I could have caught it as an oncoming pass, though it was considerably bigger than I.

Later as I retraced my footsteps, under a tree came the strangest of sounds, a rush of air indescribable. Not a swish of wings, but a continual wash of air as from a fan, or the singing edges of a wind-tunnel. Had I not seen the same eagle lifting above the treetops, I could not have imagined what could have produced such a sound.

Before the regal raptor could gain any real lift and certainly any speed, it was attacked by two redtail hawks. The eagle, being inches from the tree tops, with a seven-foot wing span, did a 180 flip, its talons suddenly skyward in its defense and then back around, with the ease and speed of a flicking wrist, before it disappeared above the lattice of tree branches.

I make a side excursion, heading up Mailbox Canyon. More wonderful woodlands, disquieting and lonesome. There are Douglas firs in these mountains, ancient of days. Sequestered pockets of pine lingering in the shadows. How many centuries have they stood alone, in canyons unvisited?

"Some trees stand while generations pass and old families last not three oaks."

The long return is uneventful, with one exception. I've an uncanny memory when it comes to landscapes and getting disoriented is a rarity, but it can happen. During the last few miles of my journey, an anxious dread befalls. I don't recognize where I am!

Three days ago when I entered these mountains, water flowed from every seam. Now, volume has been reduced in these canyons by more than half and so changed the look of the place that it's abruptly unfamiliar. I am tired. I trudged the whole day long. It's growing dark. I walk for a half hour in terrible uncertainty. Finally I find a pool of water that I'm sure of and the sense of relief is profound.

To walk a distance in the city, you give it not a thought. At the end of a day in the wilderness, you think of the miles beautiful and empty, the space that you alone have crossed. It's a little scary and equivalent to a metaphoric walk of faith. The Good Shepherd is attentive, to sheep wandered from the fold.

I rise leisurely with the morning and break camp at the same pace, blisters and sore muscles, governor gunning the engines.

Climbing out of Pipestem in more glorious sunshine. Up the green gutters beneath thirty-foot trees, over-arcing golden roofs, down steep slopes to a waiting ranch and a butte named Sombreo.

Exhausted, knocking on the door. Linda welcomes me home. She's just started there as caretaker and is busy painting interior walls, sprucing up the place after years without a woman's touch. Now glad for a break and I for a soft chair and rest.

Report on the landscapes traversed, of the noble pine forests that lay hidden beyond these desert ridges, of which she knows nothing and can scarcely believe, though she's been a San Manuel resident for years.

We are friends. In an hour we cover a lot of ground, though a more exquisite repose awaits me at home. Say good-bye, thanking her for letting me park the truck at the ranch. Leave her a tape of some of my songs. Against the odds, she wishes me success.

I climb mountains; anything is possible.

To Be Movin'

I hear my tires on the road. . . .
The wind is whistlin' my windows
Strapped to my seat. . . .
I don't care where the road goes
I've got no reason to hang around and so. . . .
I could end up in Mexico.

Now I try and keep my spirits high. . . .
Though that's sometimes hard to do
I don't know why, but it's true. . . .
I'm happy when I'm truckin' through
It's this constant battle with sameness. . . .
I think I'm losin' the fight.

Still it seems better to be movin'. . . .
Just to be movin' along.

Now from Maine to California
I've driven every road
Climbed most of the mountains. . . .
At least the ones that showed
I'll never get enough of this lovin' the road.

Love's like the diamond and love's like the flower
Love's like the wind and the rain on the water
Love's like the freedom you feel in your heart
When you drive off the mountains
And the Prairie starts.

Who'd have thought the Lord
Would have made it this way
With the mountains and towns
And the scenery that plays
In my mind at night at the close of the day.

It seems better to be movin'. . . .
Just to be movin' along

I hear my tires on the road. . . .
The wind is whistlin' my windows
Strapped to my seat. . . .
I don't care where the road goes
I've got no reason to hang around and so. . . .
I could end up in Mexico.
1978

Cerro Colorado, Pincate Preserve, Sonora Mexico.

Return to the Pinacate

I return to Mexico, more out of a need to face my fear than a desire to walk the crusty lavascapes of the Pinacate. There is a spirit that is inherent to certain landscapes; this desert leaves mine unsettled.

My cowardice dwells in the nightmare of getting the truck trapped in the sands as I did the year before. The plan this time out is to do more walking than driving. I would stroll from here to the Gulf on a whim, but I don't want to motor one inch across this terrain and become ensnared in the sand traps, that clandestinely lie in wait. When you come to this desert, you are out here all by yourself, completely alone. The prospect of getting stuck is real. It is with a great deal of trepidation that I drive across this perilous expanse of cinder and sand.

My first objective is to walk across the lavas, to the crater Cerro Colorado, appropriately named in Spanish, Red Hill. The fiery corduroy slopes flag is against the dusky desert to the southeast, as I move down the only road that leads me across the base of the volcan shield of the Pinacate.

Park the truck southwest of the red crater by some miles and start my march. The promontory appears to be on the distant horizon, in the clear desert air, perhaps unattainable before the sun goes down, but a worthy goal.

Free as I cross the open desert—well, open to the extent that I can see my destination, but there are obstacles. When the volcanoes here were active, the magma moved across the broad valley, creating a chaos of walls and terraces filled with foxholes and mini canyons, near impossible to cross and make any time doing it. Fortunately, between bouts with the rocky barrancas, there are open peppery cinder meadows where I walk unobstructed.

I cross a moonscape barren and bleak. Gossamer strands of cirrus strain the suns bright corona and a light breeze stirs wayward wands of ocotillo in the garish glare. Behind me rises the blue Pinacate. In front, the rutted rusty slopes of Cerro Colorado, as I peer into mini craters where sunken gardens of palo verde, senita cactus, and the quirky stunted elephant tree, thrive in deep eight-foot holes. Climbing in and out, up and over.

Across the cleared pastures of clinker, I leave my mark on the fragile landscape. With every crunchy step, my boots break through the crusty exterior, leaving a light brown dust in the shape of my shoes, contrasting the darkened ash. Conditions being as they are, these footprints will last a very long time, and it explains why ancient footpaths still remain.

With bullet speed, something fast and fleet disappears into a wall of palo verde, a Sonoran pronghorn. They are quite rare these days and I'm surprised and pleased to see one, though it be for all of two seconds.

The desert stretches sterile and stark, and a red hill is rising. If I didn't know, I wouldn't know, that it's the lip of a massive crater, that beyond the ruddy bluff exists a gigantic hole. The southern end of the hill is highest, a classic study in erosion, the bare slopes deeply cut by desert rain over millennia. A lancing light, catching its faceted angles in sun and shadow.

An hour and a quarter brings me to the crater's perimeter. Wonderful and odd, the outer boundary of the crater is completely devoid of plant life. Unlike the surrounding terrain filled with cactus and palo verde, nothing grows in a great ring around the red slopes. Looks like it's been purposely cleared in an unnatural way, in this nothing but a natural place. Move across the open ground heading for the lowest section of the crater's lip.

With a gathering anticipation, I go up the gentle terra-cotta slopes, ready myself for the yawning space and the bottom to drop out of the top of this hill.

On the swimming edge of a big blushed bowl, perhaps a half a mile across, maybe three-hundred feet deep, the ground falls away. Unlike the other craters in the Pinacate, which are composed of cooked coffee lavas, Cerro Colorado is unique, built of a fine-grained red brick ash. The ceramic circle, though heavily eroded, has a cheerier countenance, compared to the other murky holes that pock this desert.

Climbing down into the amphitheater, walking to the center of the ring and staring up at the circling cinnamon walls, I have walked across an empty desert, dropped into a spectacular rusted hole in the earth's crust, and I'm pleased with my accomplishment. The sense of freedom and adventure is overwhelming. But a kind of nervous apprehension about being in this bizarre landscape by myself keeps me fluttering between fear and exaltation. It is a preamble to how I always feel here in the Pinacate.

This land of desiccation is a temptress, beckoning one to abandon good sense and just wander into its empty quarters, but tempered with a perpetual ill at ease and accompanied with a loneliness that you carry about like a stone.

Here at the bottom of the bowl lies a flat pan of creosote. Apart from a mini palo verde here and there, little else grows. On the surface and in the deep groves of eroded red rock, darker rocks and pebbles lay strewn about in different patterns, collections, and populations, in the haphazard way that erosion works. But there is a master plan to this chaos, a symmetry and balance in the rocky madness. Wonder at the way rocks of different size and weight come to rest where they do.

Climb out to walk along the northern lip of the crater, which is as wide as a road and just as hard. The lowering sun is turning the bowl into a fiery furnace. The surrounding desert views are grand as well. Deep purple shades cloak the Pinacate. Ambered sunlight floods across the flat expanse to the northeast, igniting every saguaro and a million perpendicular green sticks crowd the empty space. Distant toothy sierras reflect the closing light of day.

I must hurry back to my truck, before the sun leaves me to walk this desert in the dark. Down the red slopes. Across the wide treeless perimeter that rings the crater, marching over the black lava canyons to my truck.

The sun is setting, I'm sitting on the bed of my truck, boiling water for my freeze-dried dinner. Blue shadows move across the land. A pickup approaches, down the only road that leads in or out of this lonesome disquieting desert and it makes me nervous. In my head run through the horror stories I've read and heard about the Pinacate, the ones about drug smugglers and guns, and the people who don't come back. The threatening banditos, who march out of the lavas with machine-guns, the ones who shoot first and don't care about the questions. People die out here, things happen.

Parked as I am by the side of the road, my only hope, is that we're all on the same side. The pickup has Sonoran tags and two

Mexicans ride. They roll by slowly and stare. I wave a cheerful hello, filled with a false bravado. My body language, hopefully saying . . . *yeah, I'm cool . . . you're cool. . . . I'm comfortable being here.* I pray they keep going . . . they don't.

The truck stops and the driver opens his door . . . here we go! "Do you speak Spanish?" he asks.

"No, I do not speak Spanish, I reply in a cordial manner. "You don't speak Spanish!" he repeats condescendingly. "What are you doing here? . . . Where are you going?" . . . He's walking towards me. He's got a gun strapped to his hip . . . this doesn't look good! . . . Oh, boy! . . . Here we go! . . . "I'll spend the night here, cross the Pinacate tomorrow, and sleep in Rocky Point on the Sea of Cortez tomorrow night," I say, hoping my increasing concern isn't showing.

"It is very dangerous here . . . it is not safe here . . . you should not stay," he says, in a kind of Cheech and Chong exaggerated Spanish accent. I'm not quite sure if there's a joke coming or if he's going to pull his gun. He flashes some identification I can't read. He's with the Mexican Police. He doesn't look like one. No doubt looking for the bad guys. He asks if I have a gun. They are not allowed in the Pinacate Preserve. "No," my reply. He talks of contraband, guns, and evil men. "It is so dangerous here . . . so very dangerous," he says, in his heavy accent.

What he is not saying: "You stupid gringo . . . you have no idea how much danger you're in."

He looks over my backpack with a suspicious eye, peering over my side-rail at my stove and boiling water. He's laughing at me, though it doesn't actually show. "So, you're telling me that I should leave right now?" I try to pin him down.

He walks away, getting back into his truck. "It is so dangerous," he says, in his thick Spanish-English. "Go down to Rocky Point, but don't stay here . . . it is so dangerous . . . so very dangerous," he keeps repeating. They drive off in a cloud of dust.

More has been said here than has been said, the whole incident going down in just a few moments, very odd, uncomfortable, and patronizing . . . now what?

Was this man a Guardian Angel come to warn me of impending danger, or is he busting my balls? Is something going down tonight that he knows about? Am I in the line of fire?

I know I'm in a particularly vulnerable position, camped along this road. I worried over it before this sudden apparition. I sense the messenger is right. "He that hearkeneth unto counsel, is wise."

I pack up and drive forty-five miles through the dark to Sonoyta, cross the line and sleep in a safe American campground in Lukeville, Arizona. It is New Year's Eve; fireworks celebrate my safe return.

It occurs to me that there are two deserts there in the Pinacate, a landscape over which two worlds collide. A huge empty tract of desert that straddles two countries. A large Monopoly board where a serious game of under the table economics is played out. It's a smuggler's paradise. The stakes are high and there are those willing to risk their lives and others as well, for that big elusive cash prize. The winners there win big and the losers everything. Money can be made, people are willing to try. Lives are lost in the push and pull. It has always been this way. It will remain so.

The Pinacate is also a place where Gringos like myself and other desert lovers come to see its natural wonders, to walk the lavascapes and marvel, who love it and hate it and fear it for what it is, barren and beautiful, sequestered and alone, appealing in its austere and aesthetic simplicity. Frightening, the size of a waterless waste. A dangerous land that dares the adventurer to come play chicken. The calculated risk one takes to cross it, is half its appeal.

John Audubon Jr., the son of the famous bird painter, crossed Arizona's southwestern deserts in 1850 en route to California gold. Although he lived to tell the tale, he never got over his fear of such forbidding landscape. His journey so profoundly affected his psyche that even on his deathbed, the experience ten years behind him, he ranted about the desert he could not forget, the desert the one demon he could not put to rest.

There is a spirit that is inherent to certain landscapes. The Pinacate, like those deserts for Mr. Audubon, leaves mine unsettled.

The Walk

Those leaves were turning October gold
The river ran slow with the summer grown old
Timbered shafts of sunlight
Through slots of canyon fall
Where the water spoke of time
Or was it nothing at all?

Then the wind starts to blow. . . .
Made the cottonwood sing
With the wind through their branches
Like tuning forks ring
And the raptors the same. . . .
Come the lightning and rain
Then a still small voice
Beneath the current of a storm.

"Be still and know that I am God.
I'm exalted among the nations. . . .
I'm exalted in the earth."

And with the tempests passing
Washed clean in the bright light
Where the rainbow held sway
Proceed to navigate this river
Through a carved stone hallway.

But the way that wind blew. . . .
Made the cottonwood sing
With the wind through their branches
Like tuning forks ring
And the raptors the same. . . .
Come the lightning and rain
Then a still small voice
Beneath the current of a storm.

And his words like music played
In the silent space between the thunders parade.
"I am the life . . . the truth . . . the way."

Those leaves were turning October gold
The river ran slow with the summer grown old.
1994

Aravaipa Canyon, Aravaipa Wilderness.

Aravaipa V

Yesterday's storm has washed the air clean. Rain has polished the colors of the morning and strengthened the hues of all that the now dazzling sun ignites, the dreamy greens of the cottonwood the intense blue sky. A sparkling stream path leads me into the depths of an American treasure, Aravaipa Canyon.

Aravaipa is a deep wilderness gorge of stunning beauty about seventy miles northeast of Tucson. Aravaipa Creek flows year round, a phenomenon in this desert land and water changes everything. A mini Grand Canyon, built of multi-colored, multi-tiered, thousand-foot cliff walls, that appear as wild as the day God made it. The canyon is about twelve miles in length and in the three days and two nights one is allotted by the Bureau of Land Management, the goal is to walk the canyon up and back.

It's a hikers heaven and a bird watcher's paradise, with the ever-flowing water. Hawks, eagles, and falcons fly the rocky ledges. A slue of desert song birds sing. Kingfishers, machine gun a warning ditty, as you splash through your days. Sand snipes, egrets, and herons fish the shimmering waters that support native fish populations.

Mountain lions prowl, desert bighorn sheep ascend, coatimundi, deer, coyotes, and javelina all make a comfortable living in this magnificent stone hallway.

On the southern exposed canyon walls, classic Sonoran desert flora, saguaro cactus, rock and sun. In the flood plane, groves of cottonwood, willow, ash and sycamore, interspersed with green grassy parks, cut in half by a ribbon of water. At northern walls, where the sunbeams miss their mark, grand cedars grow in the cool shadows. The upper canyon walls are built of a creamed coffee-colored rock, sometimes sprayed a light green and yellow with lichen, where water pouring off the lips of unseen plateaus, have stained the walls with black stripes, as though tar had oozed over its edges in a Utah-looking landscape.

I have walked the length of this canyon four times, exploring its major side canyons as well. Vergus Canyon is the only tributary gorge yet unexplored. I'm determined to walk it.

Much has changed since I was there last. One of my gifts is a photographic memory when it comes to landscape. Having walked a given section of land, I will almost without fault, remember the placement of every rock and tree. So it is with some surprise that I find the canyon's bottom completely rearranged.

Recent flooding has pushed through the canyon with such force that it has scoured its flooring. It has strong-armed the vast thickets of cottonwood and willow, carving new water-courses, stacking up sand-bars and reefs of river rock into small mountains. Great piles of flood debris cling to the trunks of grand old cottonwoods, rat nests of twisted trees and broken limbs, showing the high water mark to be some fifteen feet above the usual tranquil knee deep flow of stream.

I had been thinking to myself before I entered this canyon; how does a quiet stream like Aravaipa carve a canyon of this magnitude? In witnessing the aftermath of this flood's strength, it is apparent; all it takes is time.

The day deliriously sunny and warm I take my time, I haven't far to go. Five miles in, I reach Horse Camp Canyon and set up camp. There where Horse Camp enters the main gorge, sits a beautifully planted mesquite bosuqe, set in the folds of the canyon, just a few feet above the rush of water. This park is furnished with ancient cottonwood and sycamore. A lush mantel of green grass carpets the ground, filled with yellow and white spring flowers.

The place looks like the Canyon Lands of northern Arizona. Beige stone monoliths studded with cedar, where saguaro cling to walls that rise eight-hundred feet, the walls crowding the river, creating a natural cathedral.

Vergus Canyon opens up at the opposite end of the park from where I'm camped, about a half mile. That's on tomorrows itinerary. For now I head up the canyon for a place called Hell Hole, in search of desert bighorn sheep.

Without the weighty pack, my step is light. The familiar wave of euphoria sweeps over me as I drift down the canyon. This is my favorite section of Aravaipa. The compelling sculpture of the canyon walls. The marvelous color scheme of the water-stained rims.

Flowers bloom on high rock tiers, creating a light dusting of yellow snow. Increasing cloud cover forecasts a coming front. Winds rattle through the rock halls, striking the groves of cottonwood that sing like tuning forks.

I spot a tribe of coatimundi. Deer graze at every park along the way. Ducks explode off the waters. Hawks patrol canyon rims. Lion tracks cast in the gooey mud stream side.

In the same location where I discovered desert bighorn on previous visits, I search the canyon walls once more. Sure enough, they're there, this time much higher up and farther away. You can't miss the big horns and white rumps, as the small congregation dances on the stone shelves. It's a thrill to see them. To know they're here. And best to know where to look.

The first time I discovered them, it was summer. Growing tired I planted myself in the sand for a rest. After a while, I realized that one of the rocks on the opposite side of the canyon, about twenty-five yards away and perhaps fifty feet up on the first tier of ledges, had some very large horns. Six sheep stood as statues. I was thrilled.

In the first thirty minutes of observation, they never made a move, not a muscle. There were two females and three stately rams, with trophy-size horns. A lamb played on a small ledge with its protective mother. The baby appeared vulnerable but already a steady climber. Though it seemed a lion could catch an easy meal in an unwary moment, these mature rams didn't get that way by letting their guard down.

I gloried in the moment watching them graze on mesquite, slipping in and out of sight behind rocks and brush. I could not believe my good fortune. Had I sat down twenty feet on either side of my rest area, I would have missed them completely.

I walk a few more miles up the canyon, heading for Hell Hole, but it's getting late. I know a storm is coming. I'm prepared for it, but it's best to be warm and dry and in my tent when the rains come. Retrace my footsteps.

Reminiscing Hell Hole on the way back, all the side canyons there are as extraordinary as the main canyon. Hell Hole is no exception. Hundreds of feet of perpendicular sedimentary rock with strange sculpted lips, as narrow walls plunge straight down into blue shadows.

A clear, barely running stream has melted its way through solid rock, singing its way through eternity. Stately sycamores, dwarfed by the chasm's confines, glowed an eerie green, accenting the bizarre luminous walls, ignited by the slit of sky above my head.

Troops of coatimundi rained from the trees as I swung around the bends of stone. Bats bobbed in the sky window above me. Minnows drifted in the clear water pools. The sound of the rocks and gravel, like broken china under my feet, echoed off the walls, disturbing the silent sanctuary.

Caves polka-dotted the cliff walls. From perfectly carved grottoes poured springs of living water, flowing from no apparent source, out of solid rock, that gave life to ferns and flowers and color-rich mats of moss.

I know a peace, like by the streams I'm walking. The Lord I hear when nature's talking. His hand in all I see.

Back at camp, I get a good fire going and enjoy dinner. At 8:30 P.M, the rain starts and I dive into my tent. It rains hard all night long. Warm and dry in my little cocoon, I'm safe from the storm that rages just behind fragile fabric walls.

With the morning it is still raining hard. Nothing to do but sleep. Drift in and out of dreams for hours. The torrent stops about 11:30 A.M. Having logged fifteen hours in the sack, I do breakfast through the open tent door and dodge incoming raindrops.

With breakfast finished, I walk over to investigate the river. The once quiet stream is in a rage. What isn't a boiling seething rapid, is a smooth liquid conveyer belt and moves with the determined weight of an unstoppable train. That a night of rain could produce this great a transformation is a revelation. Just the water pouring out of Horse Camp and entering the main canyon, is unnerving.

Walking down to Vergus Canyon, for I had hoped to trek it, it's a complete washout. Waterfalls tumble through house-size boulders. Great trees stand midstream, trying to hold their own against the rushing current. I can barely hear myself think, above the crashing waters. Again it starts to rain. I head back to camp.

The afternoon is on and off again showers. Nowhere to go. I dare not leave the safety of the park's high ground. To cross the river would be complete foolishness. It would sweep my life away, as a leaf upon the wind. I'll have to sit tight.

Nothing beats a good storm. The alluring landscape, in which I find myself, is enhanced by the glory of the tempest. Waterfalls tumble off the dizzying heights of every canyon rim, splashing and sliding down the rock faces, adding a splendid coloring to the masterfully sculpted walls. The canyon resonates with the sound of great waters, as a hundred cataracts plunge to the river. It's like the first day of creation, the wild wet gardens of the canyon, like an Eden planted. To experience Aravaipa now and this weather is to understand how this sanctuary was fashioned, for it was born of water.

In the wilderness there is nothing but time, I spend it walking. Trapped by the water's tantrum, with nowhere to go, I realize how much time there really is. Between periodic bouts of rain and hail, stand by the river and watch the muddy waters rise.

At 4:00 P.M. another deluge begins and for two hours, a gushing torrential rain. I debate building an ark. If this keeps up, I'm going to need one. Nothing to do but sleep. I rise at 6:00 P.M. with a good omen. For fifteen minutes before the canyon grows dark, the underbelly of the cloud ceilings spark with the fire of the setting sun. The storm is losing its grip on the canyon.

Too wet for a fire, in the darkness through the open door of the tent, I cook up some oatmeal. Ring-tail cats frolic about my camp. One races right up to me within inches. They are as bold as they are beautiful.

Morning births a new day and cloaks it with a blue sky. I get up late and stake the river, that I might gauge the waters as they recede. Fortunately, the waters in Vergus have retreated a bit. I forge the currents and battle up the canyon.

Vergus walls look like those of the main canyon. But its flooring is filled with mansion-sized boulders, thrown down from the rim rock. It's a tough go, one obstacle after another. Where I can, I wade the waters and climb the boulders. Where I can't, I push up the canyon sides, pressing through impossible mesquite thickets. Forced to retreat after a distance, short of having ropes to climb the two-storied boulders, I can't get around the surging waters, or the jungles of growth.

Vergus is stunning. Water tumbles off the tawny rims above my head. White veils of water gush through every boulder barricade. The charging waters over the centuries have carved and polished deep stone gutters. Torrents dash down the rock sluices, in a joyous romp of swirl and sway. I lunch in the warm sun, beside a whizzing water slide and watch hawks float on up welling currents of air.

Back at camp, my stake on the river indicates no change in water level. The floodwaters move with a strength and resolve that deflates any daring that I thought was mine. But growing tired of this park, I brave a river crossing, for there is more room to walk and explore on the far shore.

I search for the safest crossing, deciding on the widest section with the least rapids. Swift waters are above my waist and it takes all I have to hold my own against the current. The river bottom has a life of its own, a treadmill of moving sand, rock, and gravel, that attempts to pull the rug out from under me. It's a high-wire balancing act. I make it to the other side.

I climb up Horse Camp Canyon and get the visual thrill of this excursion. Unlike Vergus, this canyon is boulder free. It's a massive stone sliding board that slips off a series of terraces. Water fills the whole of the canyon bottom and slides off big stone steps roaring like Niagara. An outstanding water show.

The force of the falling water, creating a great wind that moves down the canyon, carrying with it a billowing mist sifted from the surging waters. Rainbows strike their colors against the clouds that race by, sun showering me till I'm soaked with river rain Where water isn't tumbling, it rushes across polished rock tables heading for a fall. All plant life, be it humble grass or proud tree, bowing to the gale of wind and water.

Climbing out of Horse Camp, I walk for several miles up the main drag. With a watchful eye, I study canyon terraces, hoping to spot something move. A late afternoon sun finds mule deer sitting like statues on high grassy slopes. They hold still, thinking I don't see. The stealthy lion plays a better game of hide and seek. I settle for fresh paw prints in the mud at my feet.

I stay on the far side of the river as long as I can, but cross I must. After another long search for a safe crossing, enter again the river caldron. This time I barely make it, being pushed far downstream to reach the opposite shore.

My stake on the river indicates that the waters have actually risen through the course of the day. At dusk, I stand at the confluence of Vergus and Aravaipa and worry over the tumbling brown rapids. The water is moving with such force that it's pushing bowling ball-sized rocks along the river bottom. I can hear them striking against each other as they're swept along with the tide. There is no way I could enter these waters strapped to a backpack and survive. I may well be trapped there for a few more days.

I stoke a cozy fire and eat my last dinner. A three-quarter moon lights the canyon as though it were day. Beneath the shadows of cottonwood canopies, I stroll through the blue night. Silver moonbeams gild canyon walls that gleam like polished chrome. Despite the problems with the river, it's hard to be put out of countenance, filibustered by such beauty.

Snug in the folds of my down bag, listen to the roar of restless waters. Far above my head, I can hear somersaulting waterfalls in Horse Camp Canyon, echoing off the rock balconies, that sound like jet planes thundering, the whole canyon ajar with the quarreling voice of water.

The good Lord willing, water levels will drop. I'll brave the river tomorrow and hopefully live to tell of it.

And so it is. The river has dropped a foot by morning. For breakfast, I eat my last morsels of food; a cup of hot cocoa, five slices of salami, two slices of swiss cheese. I assess my situation and weigh my options.

One thing is certain. Having watched the weather forecast before I came, another big storm would follow the one I've just endured. Should it come before I make an escape, I could be this canyon's prisoner for a long time, without food.

Unbeknownst to myself at this very hour, the Pinal County Sheriff's Department, the Nature Conservancy Ranger for Aravaipa and Arizona Search and Rescue, are meeting outside the canyon, deciding whether to send in a helicopter for my rescue. After some deliberation they decide to wait until 5:00 P.M. to fly a copter seventy miles in from Tucson. It's a dangerous job saving the stranded from deep cut canyons, floating on the precarious winds of whirling blades. If it can be avoided, they'll do so. They decide to wait. I'm determined to conquer the river.

It's another glory day in Arizona, the sun bright and warming. A marvelous mat of lush green grass cloaks the park about my tent and is saturated with a million delicate white-and-yellow flowers.

Hawks on the hunt drift above the canyon skyline. The rivers verdant woodlands scent the air with cottonwood and willow. Colored canyon cliffs tower.

I break camp and stash my pack under a tree. To kill some time, cross the river where I did the day before and climb back in to Horse Camp to check out its tumbling Niagara. The volume still tremendous, but its flow has been reduced and that's good news. Back across the river for my pack and I'm on my way.

For a staff, I have a well-chosen piece of driftwood. I'll use it as a third leg to keep me balanced against the rushing current and cumbersome pack, also as a probing tool to search the bottom for holes. I cautiously enter the river. Make it across, just!

I walk the shores as long as I can and cross the river when I have to, each time, using all my strength, just holding my own against the swift silty torrent. Tremendous relief, having successfully crossed. Equal portions of fear and trepidation when I must once again, enter the dark swirling water. I come to see the river as an equally matched wrestling contestant. All it can throw at me and all I can muster to resist is bringing me step by step down the canyon and closer to home.

Two sections of the canyon frighten me most. Places where the walls completely close in on the river. With nothing to hold onto, the waters roll silent and deep, funneling down long corridors of stone. Having entered the hallway, there's no escape but the other end. If something goes wrong there, it would be a disaster. Strapped to a backpack, it's hard to tread water and fight this current.

Well, it's a push and a shove, this turbulent tide, but enter the hallway I do. Whirlpools, spinning and ebbing, appear and disappear, driven by powerful currents below the surface. The waist-deep waters grow progressively deeper. About halfway through, I can no longer sound the bottom with my staff. The unstoppable water is propelling me along. At the point of no return, I take a deep breath and close my eyes, fully expecting to sink to the bottom like a stone. As if by a miracle, my feet find the only high ground in this flooded hallway. Never sinking beyond my upper chest, I make it through, while all around me I cannot fathom the river's bottom with my staff.

I toil down the canyon, a few more turns, a few more bouts

142

with the river. Coming around a bend, poking my head above a large boulder to find a naked woman standing at the water's edge. Concealed as I am by the rocks, she's got my attention. I can see her back and side profile; she's looking away from me. This goddess has an outstanding figure, her large breasts floating free, her dark wet hair glistening in the sun. How beautiful the feminine form! The small of her back, the flow of leg to fanny. She stoops to splash some water.

I am in the middle of the wilderness and there's a naked woman standing right in front of me! She turns to face me, her breasts now in full view, the sun gilding her shapely wet form. My God! A naked damsel, fetching and fair! With a towel she's drying off. Unfortunately for myself, there is a mesquite tree between us, which obscures more of her than I would like. She's putting on clothes. All this going down, in about a minute, or an hour and a half, I'm not sure which.

I give her a moment to finish dressing, then swing around the rocks. Traveling not twenty feet, I'm spotted. Racing up to me like an uninhibited inquisitive child, she peppers me with a million questions. "Are you walking out of the canyon? Have you been crossing the river? How far have you come? Have you been fording these waters? Would you take us with you? Please wait! Please take us with you! Please take us with you!"

Another girl appears. Together we walk over to their camp, exchange our stories and experiences of the last few days. The storm and the rising floodwaters.

It is quickly decided that I will help them escape the canyon's confines, guiding them to safety, through tempestuous river torrents. I am a knight in shining armor, come to a maiden's distress, an answer to earnest prayer. An angel sent from heaven, commissioned of God as to their safe keeping. I'm pleased to be of service. Judging by the near panic in their eyes, I'm just what the doctor ordered.

The girls have had a rough go of it. They have been trapped in the canyon for five days. Two days before they had fallen in the river with their packs. All that they carried got soaked. With wet sleeping bags and tents, with waterlogged clothes, they struggled to keep warm and dry against the night's cold temperatures.

Caught by the stream, frightened by the river, soaked to the skin, it has not been fun.

Karen is thirty-nine years old and a seasoned backpacker. Average good looking, perhaps five seven, light brown close-cut curly hair. I have an instant rapport with her. Karen has walked in the Sierras of California, as well as the Canyon Lands in Arizona. She's walked many times in Aravaipa and is knowledgeable in horticulture and archaeology. We have much to talk about.

Pennrin is twenty-five-years old and a greenhorn, an Eastern tenderfoot. Before this outing, she had never spent a day in the wilderness. She has not had a good time. I find Pennrin attractive. She's got a good body, as I can attest having just seen it unclothed. More cute than beautiful, dark hair frames, delicate girlish features. Pennrin's whole manner reveals a childlike vulnerability that I find appealing.

The thing about wilderness backpacking, apart from the obvious beauty, is that the whole process of the walk, from the beginning to end, is a vision-quest. Tremendous physical demands are placed upon you. You are forced to make decisions. The right ones complete a successful journey, a wrong one could bring disaster. The emotional highs and lows can be extreme. In the end, a kind of revelation, but only in the end. During the whole process, it's damn hard work and it often isn't at all fun; time and again you want to just turn back, give up and go home. Only in the end, you discover of what you are physically capable and so completely renewed and refreshed in spirit, that for a week after the trial and tribulation, you are convinced that nothing is impossible in your life. But you've got to get to the end.

Pennrin has not been able to get with the program. She's been an emotional wreck for days. With the storm and waters rising, she's had a running battle with tears, bouts of depression, hopelessness, and fear. At times so despondent and desperate, as to do something foolish, like entering the river before its time or leaping from a cliff wall to end it all. This girl is on the edge.

Karen, on the other hand, has been smart enough to know that there is nothing to do but wait for the waters to recede. She's done her best to keep Pennrin calm for five days. It has not been easy. They have spelled a big "HELP" with rocks on their sandy beach, hoping helicopter would soon come. Short of that, they planned to

144

wait one more day before braving the river. Karen had shown herself the wise one.

Now with my arrival, there is a great relief. For them, a light has appeared at the end of a tunnel. Perhaps this ordeal will soon be over. Frantically, they break camp, stuffing all they have as quickly as they can into their backpacks. All of us talking at once, worrying over what obstacles lay ahead.

I give the girls a crash course in river walking. How to brace themselves against the rushing current. How to plant their feet for sure footing, on a river bottom that stays in continuous motion.

It's no wonder the girls were so intimidated by this part of the river, trying unsuccessfully in several spots to cross. What isn't over my head is a rapid so swift and strong I can't stand against it.

One option is to climb on a ledge a few feet above the river, clinging to a sheer rock wall that crowds the deep water pools, balancing myself on this shelf for a few feet, then dropping in on waters where I hope they won't be over my head, this being rather difficult with a cumbersome pack. Before I drop over the ledge and disappear from the girls' view, I tell them to sit tight. "If it's safe and I can cross the river, I'll be back for you. Just sit tight! I'll be back!" I vanish behind the rocks.

I lower myself into waters that are above my belt, struggling to the other side. I take off my pack and head back for the girls. As I look across the water, Pennrin is on the ledge and ready to drop in on the river. The look on Pennrin's face is one of absolute terror. Paralyzed by fear, she cries out, in this helpless, vulnerable, panic-stricken voice, the pure desperate sound of which I will not soon forget. "Don't leave, us, Drew! . . . Please don't leave us!" This girl is on the edge.

I race to her side, assuring her that won't happen. She drops into the drink and clinging like a cocklebur, we move across the water as one. Planting Pennrin firmly on the opposite shore, I head back for Karen and we too make the crossing.

Crossing the river there was big hurdle. Sometimes just getting started is the hardest part. We're on our way down the canyon, walking on the shores where we can, crossing the river when we have to.

Pennrin is so excited at the prospect of getting out of this five-day ordeal, she can't get out of the canyon fast enough. When on firm ground, she is practically running down the beach to the next crossing. Then waiting pensively by the scary swirling water, where we all cross together. The girl is on the edge.

Karen, on the other hand, hurt her leg on the first crossing, not badly, but she's bringing up the rear. I'm in between, trying to keep the two ends of this line tied.

We ford the fearsome waters together. I lead the way, probing the boiling currents with my staff. They, holding onto each other, hold onto me. Sometimes we get halfway across and are forced to retreat, in search of safe waters. Calmly, methodically, we make our precarious journey down the canyon.

The ladies have put me in a wonderful position. They cannot stop thanking me for having come to their rescue. All that I would like to be, they believe I am. They have picked up on my steady, rock-calm demeanor. They constantly flatter, telling me how brave I am. They can't believe how unruffled I appear, under such stressful conditions, that as a savior I have come for them. They have put their complete faith and trust in me and this with a total abandon, as only a child can. They adoringly hang onto my every word. A mega boost for the ego. They have given me a power, I have rarely experienced so consummately. Thrilled to be of service.

The last big hurdle, the place I feared the most. The second great hallway of sheer rock walls, forming an inescapable corridor. So intimidating was the look of the water as it funneled down the long deep hallway, it gave us all a start. Marching along in single file like elephants, each holding the tail of the one before. The unstoppable water shot us through the stone chute, like bullets through a rifle barrel, landing at the end of the lengthy passage way unscathed, the worst of the river behind us.

With a few more turns of canyon and a few more river crossings, we reach the mouth of the canyon. We have made it. Here walls retreat to broaden the valley. The river, now less restricted, is less threatening. Two miles to our cars and home.

In the mists of one of our river crossings, we look up from the umbered waters to see three people approaching. These strangers seem mighty glad to see us! We say hello and make our introductions.

Ted Grooms is a rancher who lives at the mouth of Aravaipa. Working closely with the Nature Conservancy, he has been in on our planned rescue all day. A helicopter has been flown in from Tucson. At 5:00 P.M., just twenty minutes from now, it will fly up the canyon to save us from the floodwaters. Ted started up the canyon to see if we might be coming. Now, having found us, he suggests we hurry along and try to catch the copter before it takes off.

Mr. Grooms is as nice a guy as you would ever hope to meet, an engaging handsome blond, with a winning bright smile. Electric blue eyes peer out from under the rim of a fabulous green Australian safari hat, with a black-and-white checkered flannel shirt that complements his now wet khaki pants. Luscious leather boots, the kind I'd give my eye-teeth for. He is without doubt Arizona's best-dressed rancher. Looks as if he's just stepped out of the pages of an L L Bean catalog.

Everyone is talking at once. They, because we have been found, are asking us more questions than we can answer about our ordeal. And we, having been sequestered in this canyon, for what seems a near eternity, inquire of news from the outside world.

Ted had brought along two ranch guests; Mark and his eighteen-year-old son, Kevin. All want to know what wildlife we have seen and how we managed to escape unscathed, the turbulent waters.

Ted explains that in the years he has been living there, he has never seen the Galiuro Mountains so packed with snow. The storm we had weathered, had deposited a thick wintry blanket of the white, on the plateaus beyond these towering cliffs that now confine us. The authorities were concerned that the 80-degree days would melt the snows so quickly, that the river would rise even higher, making a difficult situation worse.

Awash in a brilliant blast of late afternoon sun, we make our last river crossing. Climbing up a small bluff, across a large fenced field, terraced above the muddled waters and heading for the ranch house. Flowering cottonwood forests have sent a billion floater seeds to drift in the pure air, a blizzard of tiny round feathers, beneath sincere blue desert skies.

Six of us string out across the wide field. Pennrin and I bring up the rear. She confides in me how frightening this experience has been for her. How out of hope she had reached the depths of despair. How desperate her prayers, how lost she felt when help didn't come. How as an angel of mercy, I had appeared in their mists.

At the end of the field, we climb a steep hill on the top of which sits Ted's ranch house. As we labor up the sharp rise, a red helicopter whizzes over our heads, moving up the canyon on its mission to save us. Waving our arms, we signal the pilot that all is OK. Making a big loop, he gives us a wave and heads seventy miles back to Tucson.

The ranch has a commanding view of Aravaipa Canyon. It's a surprise to see the Galiuros layered in deep snow and it moving all the way down to the terraces above the river, while the cottonwoods of the river bottom are August green. It was quite storm. A majestic landscape made all the more appealing with the addition of snow.

We pile into Ted's Land Rover, for the short ride to our waiting cars. In the parking lot, we meet the Nature Conservancy Ranger for Aravaipa Canyon and a Sheriff from the Pinal County Sheriff's Department. They ask us the obvious questions. They make sure that we're all right, though I can tell they are a little pissed off that we have put them to so much trouble. We apologize and thank them for their concern. All is well that ends well.

In closing, the ranger related his adventure of the day before. Knowing the river was on the rise and concerned for our safety; he battled up the canyon in hopes of finding us. In the long stone corridor that filled us with dread, in waters shoulder deep, he was forced to retreat. He knew then that we were in trouble and was frightened for us. He began planning the helicopter rescue.

Karen wants to treat me to dinner. It's decided we'll stop at a Mexican eatery in the small town of Mammoth as we venture home to Tucson. The drive out of the canyon is spectacular. The rugged Galiuros, snow-filled. The desert floor, a patchwork quilt of striking blue lupines that rug the hillsides with color. Lavender air hangs over remote, white mountains that trail into the distance.

From a booth in La Castillia, we peer through the picture windows across the San Pedro River to the snow-filled Galiuros. We discuss our timely escape from Aravaipa. It's been a real adventure. Compliments continue. "Oh, Drew, you're so brave . . . so strong . . . so steady." I would like to believe them. One is rarely placed in the situation where help is so desperately needed. I've gotten more out of this than they. Humbled and honored to be of service.

With dinner complete we say good-bye. The euphoric drive

back to Tucson. Through the dark and the flicker of headlights. I can see tumbling cataracts as they pour off canyon rims in the morning after the storm. Desert Bighorn Sheep dancing on high rock ledges. The roaring Niagara, in Horse Camp Canyon. Those scary determined floodwaters. The absolute terror, in Pennrin's eyes, when she would cross the river. Fearless ringtail cats that wandered my darkened campsite. Fresh lion tracks pressed into gooey brown mud. Deer silently watching from green stream-side parks.

Aravaipa is magnificent. Wouldn't have missed the storm for anything. The fact that I have conquered its flood waters and lived to tell the tale, has made it all the more rewarding; a vision-quest complete.

A Long Way to Go Before I'm Home

Tall blue mountains stand. . . .
These prairies they roll green
Braided silver threads a river runs
A distant city shines . . . beyond the distant sun
With a long, long way to go, before I'm home.

Sailors man their ships. . . .
On great waters ply their trade
A captain steers by faith for stars
Alone to chart this wilderness. . . .
I chase the dream I made
With a long, long way to go, before I'm home.

Let the storm roll in . . . let the river waters rise
Fill those high mountain meadows with snow
Angels I believe. . . .
They've been whisperin' in my ears
Keeping fears and dangers at bay
Now I've got to say . . . you ought to know
Home's a long, long way to go.

Tall blue mountains stand. . . .
These prairies they roll green
Braided silver threads a river runs
A distant city shines . . . beyond the distant sun
With a long, long way to go, before I'm home.

Just a long, long way to go, before I'm home.
1991

Chollas, Organ Pipe, and the Bates Mountains.

The Walk Out

Something happens to the spirit when it tests itself against mountains and revelation at its culmination.

Deeper than canyons, older than mountains, I would that I had wings.

I would that I had wings and appear like an angel at the top of a ridge. Walking blue corrugations, over forested mountains, into the depths of lonesome canyons, to light by streams, beneath whispering fir canopies, finding a rest and a joy in the work of His hands and a peace beyond this beauty, deeper than canyons, older than mountains.

I would that I had wings.

I write this at the end of an arc of walking. From the Chisos Mountains along the Big Bend in Texas, to the lavascapes of the Pinacate in Mexico, from the basilicas of Zion in Utah, to the endless forests of the Leopoled Wilderness in New Mexico, across the Mogollon Rim, to the red rock cathedrals in Sedona. From the Kaibab Plateau, across a Grand Canyon to the peaks near Flagstaff and south to Patagonia. From the Kofa Mountains in the west to the Chiricahuas in the east. I've left few stones unturned.

I have shared here but a few of my walks and a few of my songs, concentrating on my own backyard. And in reviewing my journals, I see less is more. Another story becomes one more magnificent indistinguishable canyon. A dreamscape is like that. Exceptional Arizona is less a place on a map than a geography of the spirit.

For the Southwest is at least as much a place in my head as it is a place in reality. But the reality is so rewarding and it is the foundation on which I have set a large portion of my life.

All I ever wanted to do was to write songs and take a walk somewhere. The world is not interested in such craziness. Walking Arizona has provided an unending adventure and a wellspring of song-writing inspiration. It is a place steeped in an eternal beauty, an undying mystery. It is a theater for the imagination. I have let my feet and my mind wander.

I am the least practical person I ever met, as evidenced from the fact that I am on my fourth decade of writing songs, with the full knowledge that no amount of talent, determination or dogged pursuit of my goal can bring this dream to fruition as a working reality. I remain undaunted for one reason only. It is a natural calling; I wouldn't know who I was if I couldn't pick up a guitar. I have pursued my craft with an honest and pure heart, for the sheer love and joy of doing it.

I have pursued walking with the same enthusiasm, for the same reasons. It is a natural calling; I wouldn't know who I was if I couldn't take a walk. For me there has always been an inherent emotional and spiritual response to landscape, which pulls me into it like gravity. I am so enamored with the artful allure of land forms, it is nothing short of a religious experience. Any interesting landscape would do. Preferably a Western landscape. But if I lived in Scotland or Spain in Appalachia or Argentina or name the place, my life would be the same. I would be walking and fashioning songs. The walking and the writing go hand in hand like a marriage.

The adventure of walking lends itself to romanticism. The glory of creation lends itself to spiritual inspiration. The act of walking brings a clear mind. My natural joyous response to all this beauty is a spontaneous melody.

Fortunately, the artist has license to create out of things around him, that which he will. Living in Arizona has given me a lot to work with, a large and diverse canvas from which to draw. But the wonderful world I have created in my own imagination is at least as real as the real wonderful world, and sometimes it's quite hard for me to distinguish between the two. Perhaps it doesn't matter.

Sadly there are things I dislike about the place as well, things I wish I could change, but my impractical artistic outlook allows me to overlook the unpleasant and see only the beautiful. The futility of writing songs, now and then, comes and slaps me upside the head, and this disquieting realization, proves to me how much I am living in a province of my own fabrication and how much there is I cannot reconcile.

Though Arizona remains an extraordinary place for an extraordinary number of reasons and for all those reasons, I love it with my whole heart. Its history, ancient and new, its people, the blend of cultures, architecture, religion, Gods handiwork on a grand and diversified scale, the amorous smell of it when it rains. I was born for the place. I am certain that if you took out of the equation my love for singing and writing songs, this walking, and Arizona itself, my life would cease to exist, at least as I have known it or ever wanted it to be.

And the physical and emotional high that comes, with the march and the miles, is an intoxication born of enchanting beauty that encompasses and what happens to the spirit over time, as you participate with intricate landscapes like these. There is revelation in walking, and under these conditions, any man can find himself. It's that still small voice that I've been listening for. It's led me out of this door and down these roads. And having reached this physical plateau, although tired, there seems no limit to my ability to walk endlessly onward.

However, after two decades plus of the habitual hinterland plod, I fear there may be somatic limits to how far one can walk, or even needs to. With the strength of my better years behind me, I carry battle scars as a result of the hard-won miles, arthritic knees, and a deteriorating will. Though I pray the Good Lord gives me the brawn to continue, for I literally would not know who I was if I couldn't take a walk. And my life and music never make more sense than when returning from a good jaunt. But I've done my job, climbing every canyon ridge and peak and I've loved every aching moment.

I can close my eyes and drift up a hundred extraordinary canyons, over every mountaintop, across deep valleys, impassable rivers, to a resting place in the quiet hills.

And of course, I have a million memories. Bright reverent mornings, brilliant afternoons spent in a glorious sun, the resplendent sky embers of evening, never the same, clear nights filled with campfires and a billion distant suns, traipsing abandoned dry dusty deserts, strolling enchanted mountain forests, forging diamond rivers, sauntering prairies rolling perfect, listening for psalms in tabernacled canyons.

I know of secret springs in the mountain passes. Where clandestine waters tumble through a canyon's crinkle. Where large fish drift like dirigibles in deep water pools. Where carved color-rich stilettos of stone stare down on belittled groves of cottonwood, never visited. Of covert timbers, that have been aging for a thousand years in the clefts of confidential canyons. It seems I know every nook and cranny. I can float in and out of these locations at will and often do.

I see art, I see great beauty, I see the divine in natural things. I know a peace, like by the streams I'm walking, the Lord I hear when natures talking. His hand in all I see.

Being Swedenborgian in my outlook explains quite a bit.

My purpose in writing was simply an excuse to talk about beautiful things, the art of this creation, and a passing note on the spiritual implications of landscape. And this thought has so enhanced my appreciation of nature and has lifted my mind above the merely natural things placed before me, which in and of themselves are marvelous and remarkable beyond words.

In short, there is an inherent spiritual correspondence, with the natural formation, which is a metaphor reflecting a deeper spiritual reality.

Apart from the singularly striking and uncommon components that make this a magical place. I love Arizona first and foremost, for the art of the place, the sheer esthetics of this creation. For I dream of Western skies, the color of the air, and the light in the canyons. That bend in the river where the cottonwood grows, that's where my memory flows, and my heart it won't leave. I am less an artist than I am one who appreciates good art and sees it in most everything. From the exultant to the mundane, everything in my eye has an aesthetic, purposeful balance. And like all good art, everything is wrapped in metaphor and the more I look, the more I see.

The very act of walking is its own metaphor and is analogous to a walk of life, with profound spiritual implications, and a potent parable, when walking across a desert to a point of water.

For Arizona is just a pile of rocks, though it be a beautiful pile of rocks. And if beauty was all that could be found here, that would be enough on which to be content. I remain convinced that there is more to this than meets the eye, that the things placed before us are representative of deeper spiritual realities not always apparent.

If, "Nature is the art of God," to quote Thomas Brown, then landscape is saturated with spiritual metaphor. For what artist

155

worth his salt could be satisfied with painting just the natural objects he sees, but in using these things, to tell a deeper story.

Undoubtedly, there is more to God than I'll ever know. But in regards to the art of landscape, I remain certain that nothing works as well as creation and does not have God in it.

Surely the Greatest Artist, the source from which all things spring, and in whom we live and move and have our being, has fashioned nature in such a way, apart from the obvious purposeful practicalities of creation and if understood in its proper light, as a kind of spiritual metaphor, to reveal a higher truth. If we could lift this material veil, we would then see clearly, that in every created thing, there is something reflecting our creator, his purpose and ourselves as well. For God is a perfect man and we are in his image. Everything fashioned reflects this truth. "Therefore, all nature, is a theater representative of the Lord's Kingdom."

Sometimes until a statement is made on a given subject, it doesn't become a tangible idea on which the mind can rest.

Just as music is pure emotion put to melody and the emotional response to it moves us to the core of our being, as great art lifts the spirit and the mind of man to a higher purpose, beyond himself, so the art of this creation is doing the same. And this spiritual tugging at our hearts and this emotional response to beautiful things, as when we stand by a river, or walk through a forest, or look up at the mountain, is both a conscious and unconscious, reciprocal interplay, between the creator and the created.

"If mountains reflect celestial love and the hills below them, the spiritual; if natural water corresponds to spiritual truth; if rocks signify faith; if animals, reflect varying affections and the trees, perception and knowledge; if birds, intellectual things; if gardens, groves and parks, intelligence," then landscape becomes a stage on which everything is a metaphor reflecting his purpose, like an image in a mirror, a place where natural mountains and rivers, are spirit condensed.

This grand sweep and wide array of diversified landscapes, that Arizona has to offer, makes this school of thought all the more dramatically pronounced and poignant.

Is it possible to walk across a desert land and upon discovering a seep or a spring or a flowing river, not be impressed by the resonant spiritual implications of such a phenomenon? Not in the trappings themselves, which are wonderful and remarkable, but in what ethereal substance they represent. This celestial component, the ingredient that satisfies, and a truth that wends me on my way.

And so, I remain captivated by the intricate tapestry that is Arizona. I am drawn by the sheer weight of its beauty and this tangible, spiritual correspondence, to walk this Gloryland. The aesthetically pleasing and comprehensive sweep of this creation. Its worthless creosote deserts, the symmetry of its forested mountain skylines, its graceful prairies, its shining rivers, the proportionate arrangement of these contrasting parts. The pleasing impression of its size, colors, and forms, have come to rest on my mind like a melody . . . with a melody in mind.

So I won't belabor the point. If things are beautiful just because they are beautiful, then so be it. But I am so intensely and affectionately moved by this splendid artful creation and I can't help but see deeper spiritual things within, the more I gaze into this natural painting. This pleases my spirit no end and makes me think and ponder beautiful things.

Something happens to the spirit when it tests itself against mountains and revelation at its culmination.

Deeper than canyons, older than mountains, I would that I had wings.

I would that I had wings and appear like an angel at the top of the ridge. Walking blue corrugations, over forested mountains, into the depths of lonesome canyons, to light by streams, beneath whispering fir canopies, finding a rest and a joy in the work of His hands and a peace beyond this beauty, deeper than canyons, older than mountains.

I would that I had wings.

Stone Altars, Wilderness of Rocks, Santa Catalina Mountains.

Snow on the Santa Catalinas

It snowed on the Santa Catalinas today
Bright sun on the clouds as they faded away
Left the snow line high above the desert floor.

I'll hate to leave this place. . . .
I'll hate to leave this town
I'll hate to go back home
And stop this wanderin' around
I've got to go back east. . . .
I've got some work to do
If my words could really tell ya. . . .
I just hate to leave you.

In the spring there's a flower on everything
Arizona has this smell. . . .
You grab your girl and you dream
At night a soft warm breeze up from old Mexico.

I'll hate to leave this place. . . .
I'll hate to leave this town
I'll hate to go back home
And stop this wanderin' around
I've got to go back east. . . .
I've got some work to do
In the canyons in the east
Where I'll be workin'
I'll be dreamin' of you.

You were the clouds that Rincon mornin'
Crashin' into the mountains
As the thundershowers came
I didn't catch or heed the warnin'
Started lookin' for some shelter
But got caught out in the rain
When I finally found some rocks to house me
I hid there till the rainbow came.

159

I'll hate to leave this place. . . .
I'll hate to leave this town
I'll hate to go back home
And stop this wanderin' around
I've got to go back east. . . .
I've got some work to do.

Now you can keep the city, there's nothin' for me there
Give me a stretch of open desert, and I don't much care
Still can't say what I want, but hope to find it there.

I'll hate to leave this place. . . .
I'll hate to leave this town
I'll hate to go back home
And stop this wanderin' around
I've got to go back east. . . .
I've got some work to do.

It snowed on the Santa Catalinas today.
1979

Blessed Beyond Measure

Every day it's the same old thing
I climb into these canyons
And I sing . . . sing . . . sing.

I'm blessed beyond measure. . . .
With family and friend. . . .
And a dream each day to work on
There are mountains to climb. . . .
And the fun never ends
I'm blessed beyond measure, my friend. . . .
Blessed beyond measure.

I'm blessed with the morning. . . .
The black night all stars
And a new dawn to start my day in
With this glorious sun on my sill come to play
I'm blessed beyond measure that way.

I'm blessed beyond measure
To follow that which I love
And there's joy in the fields I'm working
But unto summits abiding a sojourner tends
I'm blessed beyond measure, my friend. . . .
Blessed beyond measure.

I'm blessed with the calling. . . .
The promised glory that waits
And the storms through the sylvan valley
For the carols I hear and the songs that I play
I'm blessed beyond measure that way.

Don't break the spell of my inspiration. . . .
Don't take away the dream
An epiphany waiting in the mountains. . . .
Reveled in the river and the sunlight beam.

Make every day the same old thing
I'll climb into these canyons
And I'll sing . . . sing . . . sing.

I'm blessed beyond measure. . . .
With family and friend. . . .
And a dream each day to work on
There are mountains to climb. . . .
And the fun never ends
I'm blessed beyond measure, my friend. . . .
Blessed beyond measure.

'Cause every day it's the same old thing
I climb into these canyons
And I sing . . . sing . . . sing.
1997

Credit Where Credit is Due

This book and many of my songs could not have been written over the years without the continued insight and inspiration derived from author John C. Van Dyke (1856–1935) who wrote with such artful eloquence about *The Desert,* who showed me how wonderful words might be cobbled together in praise of beautiful things. An art critic who explained in a tangible way what I knew instinctively and yet did not completely recognize, until of course he wrote it down, what it was that my aching heart so loved about this Gloryland. His observant eye and admirable prose cannot go unmentioned here, for he in the end is the real artist in this book.

I have also been profoundly moved by the Swedish philosopher and theologian, Emanuel Swedenborg (1688–1772). His theory of "Spiritual Correspondence" I have alluded to in this book. The quotes in "Beautiful Things" and "The Walk Out," are his.

Ralph Waldo Emerson described Swedenborg: "A colossal soul . . . who lies vast abroad on his times, uncomprehended by them. . . . One of the mastodons of literature, he is not to be measured by whole colleges of ordinary scholars."

Henry James, Sr. wrote: "The incomparable depth and splendor of Swedenborg's genius are shown in this, that he alone of men has . . . dared to bring creation within the bonds of consciousness. . . . He grasped with clear and intellectual vision the seminal principles of things."

Hellen Keller called him a "Titan Genius . . . an eye among the blind, an ear among the deaf."

I have thrilled to his theology and believe it worthy of investigation, both by the believer and non-believer, the scientist and the intellectual, or a simple man of faith such as myself.

Just as John C. Van Dyke taught me to see that the landscape itself is a painting, Emanuel Swedenborg taught me to see that the artist, who is so exquisitely manipulating this natural canvas, is the spirit of God himself.

For more information on Emanuel Swedenborg, write: Swedenborg Foundation, 320 North Church Street, West Chester, Pennsylvania 19380. Phone (610) 430-3222. The e-mail address is info@swedenborg.com.

There is a great old English expression: some trees stand while generations pass and old families last not three oaks. I found it appropriate and apropos for "Pipestream Canyon."

Along the way I've thrown in a few Bible verses for good measure.

All songs were written by me, with the exception of "Far Trails." These lyrics I share with Henry Herbert Knibbs. I do not know of this man and his accomplishments, or even how I stumbled on to his words, but when I was working on this song, I came upon his lines, "Far trails await me," which fit perfectly into the melodic change I had already written. An immaculate match that finished the song, and the rest, as they say, is unrecognized history.

"Hill Tops High and Fair" is an anonymous poem that I discovered in *Streams in the Desert*, a compilation of inspirational writings by Mrs. Charles E. Cowman, published by the Oriental Missionary Society in 1946. It spoke to me immediately, not just because of its sentiments, but because it expressed it in a way that I would not have imagined expressing it. Even good poetry rarely makes a good song. I added a few lines of my own to make it one, and it remains one of my favorites.

"Patagonia" and "To Be Movin' " have been published by Vincent Montana Jr. Music ASCAP, 1981, all rights reserved.

If I could spell, I would consider myself an educated man. Sadly, this is not the case. I thank Daisy Willeford, long-time resident of San Manuel and the San Pedro River Valley, not only for her wonderful stories about the Galiuro Mountains, but also for her assistance with this manuscript and in helping me get a few things right.

I thank the Good Lord for just about everything else, for the freedom and strength to walk this Gloryland. For the loving and supportive fortunate family I was born into. For warm friends found, who have shared the dreams of songs and the glory of mountains.